'You' and 'Thou' in Shakespeare

Arden Performance Companions

Series Editors: Michael Dobson, Abigail Rokison-Woodall and
Simon Russell Beale

Published titles
Shakespearean Rhetoric, by Benet Brandreth
Shakespeare and Meisner, by Aileen Gonsalves and Tracy Irish

Further titles in preparation
Shakespeare and Laban, by Jacquelyn Bessell and Laura Weston

Arden Performance Editions

Series Editors: Michael Dobson, Abigail Rokison-Woodall and
Simon Russell Beale

Published titles
A Midsummer Night's Dream, edited by Abigail Rokison-Woodall
Hamlet, edited by Abigail Rokison-Woodall
Macbeth, edited by Katherine Brokaw
Much Ado About Nothing, edited by Anna Kamaralli
Othello, edited by Paul Prescott
Romeo and Juliet, edited by Abigail Rokison-Woodall
Twelfth Night ,edited by Gretchen Minton

Further titles in preparation
As You Like It, edited by Nora Williams
The Tempest, edited by Miranda Fay Thomas

Arden Performance Companions

'You' and 'Thou' in Shakespeare

A Practical Guide for Actors, Directors, Students and Teachers

Penelope Freedman

THE ARDEN SHAKESPEARE
LONDON • NEW YORK • OXFORD • NEW DELHI • SYDNEY

THE ARDEN SHAKESPEARE
Bloomsbury Publishing Plc
50 Bedford Square, London, WC1B 3DP, UK
1385 Broadway, New York, NY 10018, USA
29 Earlsfort Terrace, Dublin 2, Ireland

BLOOMSBURY, THE ARDEN SHAKESPEARE and the Arden Shakespeare logo
are trademarks of Bloomsbury Publishing Plc

First published in Great Britain 2021

Series design by Charlotte Daniels
Cover image © Max Saeling / Unsplash

A catalogue record for this book is available from the British Library.

A catalog record for this book is available from the Library of Congress.

ISBN: HB: 978-1-3501-1868-3
       PB: 978-1-3501-1867-6
       ePDF: 978-1-3501-1869-0
       eBook: 978-1-3501-1870-6

Series: Arden Performance Companions

Typeset by RefineCatch Limited, Bungay, Suffolk
Printed and bound in Great Britain

To find out more about our authors and books visit www.bloomsbury.com
and sign up for our newsletters.

For Robert, as always
'For others say thou dost deserve, and I
Believe it better than reportingly.'

Contents

Series preface

The Arden Performance Companions offer practice-focussed introductions to different aspects of staging Shakespeare's plays: whether accounts of how Shakespearean drama may respond to particular systems of rehearsal and preparation, guides to how today's actors can understand and use different facets of Shakespeare's verbal style, or explorations of how particular modern practitioners have used Shakespeare's scripts as starting points for their own embodied thinking about the social and aesthetic possibilities of popular theatre.

The premise of this series is that the interpretation of Shakespeare is not confined to the literary analysis of his scripts, but also includes their rehearsal and performance. With this in mind, the Arden list of editions of Shakespeare expanded in 2017 to include not only heavily-annotated scholarly texts of each play, designed primarily for use in colleges and universities, but a new series, the Arden Performance Editions of Shakespeare, designed primarily for use in rehearsal rooms and at drama schools. Just as academic editions of Shakespeare may be supplemented by books introducing students to different modes of academic criticism, so these Arden Performance Companions seek to supplement the Arden Performance Editions, offering a rich variety of practical guidance on how Shakespeare's plays can be brought to life in contemporary performance.

Acknowledgements

My sincere thanks to my fellow Playcraft members, and to the Gulbenkian Theatre at the University of Kent for the delight of directing and performing Shakespeare over the course of twenty-five years.

Thanks, too, to students at The Shakespeare Institute, University of Birmingham, for exploring these texts and experimenting with these ideas. Their responses have been invaluable in the writing of this book.

Notes on texts

All the extracts from the plays are taken from the *Arden Shakespeare Complete Works*.

The extracts used are intended for experimentation and the aim has been to make them as user-friendly as possible. To that end, a number of them have been abridged in order to keep the focus on the you/thou patterns and reveal them more clearly.

1

Introduction

In *The Taming of the Shrew*, Petruchio starts his wooing of Katherine with:

> Hearing **thy** mildness praised in every town,
> **Thy** virtues spoke of and **thy** beauty sounded,
> Yet not so deeply as to **thee** belongs,
> Myself am moved to woo **thee** for my wife.
>
> (*Taming of the Shrew*, 2.1.192–5)

But he ends it with:

> And will **you**, nill **you**, I will marry **you**.
>
> (*Taming of the Shrew*, 2.1.265)

Why does he make the change? What is the difference between **thou, thee, thy, thine** on the one hand, and **you, your, yours**[1] on the other? Does it matter?

Shakespeare's audiences clearly understood a difference: letters and trial transcripts of the sixteenth and seventeenth centuries show ordinary people using and exploiting the implications of choosing to

---

[1] **Thou** is the *subject* form (**Thou** art my love), **thee** is the *object* form (I love **thee**) **and thy/thine** are *possessives*.

call someone '**you**' or to call them '**thou**'. Those implications were part of the small change of the language of the time and they were naturally incorporated into the language of the plays of the time. To call someone **you** or **thou** was as important as the name by which you addressed them – title, surname, Christian name or nickname. It revealed attitude and relationship in everyday life and on stage.

As modern audiences, readers, students, teachers, actors or directors, we are the poorer for being deaf to the differences between **you** and **thou** and ignorant of their implications. If we think about them at all, we often assume that **thou** is more formal than **you**: we connect it with the language of the Bible, hymns and prayers, and nineteenth-century poetry. The first surprise for students and actors is to discover that **thou** was generally *less* formal, more intimate and personal, the pronoun used between lovers, close friends, parents and children.

The reasons lie in the history of **you** and **thou**. Up until the thirteenth century, **thou** was the only way to address one person and **you** was used only when addressing more than one. With the Norman Conquest came a French-speaking upper class and, as the French influence began to spread into the English language, English speakers began to imitate the French habit of using their plural, **vous**, as a polite, respectful singular in place of the more intimate **tu**. So, from the thirteenth century onwards, **you** started being used in the singular as well as the plural. It was a special usage, aping courtly language, intended for expressing particular politeness and respect. However, it quickly spread down the social strata and though, for a while, **thou** continued to be the normal or 'default' singular, the use of **you** rapidly became more common until, by the sixteenth century, it had actually replaced **thou** as the normal singular, and **thou** had become the unusual form.

By the time Shakespeare was writing, then, **you** was the ordinary, unexceptional, neutral form, while **thou** was now unusual, 'marked', and carried a rather divergent range of special meanings. It is appreciating the 'specialness' of **thou** that is the key to understanding the way Shakespeare and his contemporaries used it.

- **Thou** was used to close friends, lovers, family members and children; it was, in other words, the informal, intimate form of address.

- **Thou** was used by the aristocracy to patronize social inferiors, servants and so on, and they were addressed with respectful **you** in return.

- **Thou** was used for insults, and to express anger or contempt; it marked the deliberate refusal to use **you**, the choice not to be polite.

One way of making sense of these apparently contradictory uses is to see **you** as the public pronoun, the form of address that included a person's many roles and faces (in this sense, it retained something of its plural origins). **Thou**, then, was used when intimacy and affection made this public recognition unnecessary (rather like using a nickname or pet name), but it was also used to cut someone down to size, to treat them as though they were a social inferior, to refuse them the dignity of their public roles, to address them with insulting directness. This kind of use is made overt in *Twelfth Night* in Sir Toby Belch's advice to Sir Andrew Aguecheek when he is writing his challenge to 'Cesario': charging him to be 'curst' and to 'taunt' him, he adds: 'If **thou thou'st** him some thrice, it shall not be amiss' (*Twelfth Night*, 3.2.44).

The use of **thou** and **you** was very flexible. We find, both in the language of ordinary people and in the plays, rapid shifts between the two, sometimes in the same sentence or line of verse. These shifts to reflect transitory mood changes are what make paying attention to the pronouns so revealing. They act as a kind of barometer: where we find increasing **thou** use, there we find a rise in the emotional temperature, whether the emotion be love, fury, contempt or grief. Looking at **you** and **thou** patterns helps to clarify uncertain relationships, to track the dynamics of a scene, to identify crisis moments.

In fact, even without analysing the implications of **thou**, many actors respond instinctually, almost viscerally, to the feel of it in the mouth. Its vocal characteristics, the lingual consonant and the front vowel, lend themselves to both its functions: it can be caressed seductively on the tongue by a lover, but equally it can spit anger and contempt. It is a gift to an actor.

Within the broad categories of intimacy/affection and anger/ contempt there are further, fascinating patterns to be found. Summarized below are the patterns to be found in Shakespeare's plays (though it should be emphasized at this point that Shakespeare was not alone in using the pronouns in this way: these were the conventions of the time, and the same patterns are found in the work of his contemporaries).

- Men use **thou** far more commonly than women do: they use it not only to assert power and status and for angry altercations, but also to express male bonding and affection. Women use **thou** to one another far less: thus, for example, Benedick and Claudio in *Much Ado About Nothing* use **thou** to each other but Beatrice and Hero do not.

- It is men who initiate **thou** address as lovers. It is the pronoun for the wooer who believes that his love is, or will be, reciprocated: Romeo uses it to Juliet from the outset, as does Petruchio, perversely, to Katherine, in spite of her protests – it is one of the ways he wrong-foots her. Benedick, once he starts wooing Beatrice, wavers uncertainly between **thou** and **you**. Rejected lovers, like Silvius with Phebe in *As You Like It*, or Proteus with Silvia in *The Two Gentlemen of Verona*, use **you**.

- For a woman to use **thou** to a potential lover before he has used it to her is a mark of inappropriate or forward behaviour. We see both Goneril and Regan use it to Edmund in *King Lear*, though he does not reciprocate, and we see Olivia use it to Viola (as Cesario) in *Twelfth Night*, and Titania use it to Bottom in *A Midsummer Night's Dream*, both of them in the throes of comically unsuitable passions. Respectable women use **thou** sparingly.

- **Thou** is the pronoun for mutual lovers, but they tend to use it only when expressing their love. When they move to other topics, they revert to **you**. Romeo and Juliet are unique in using it throughout the play; no other pair of lovers uses it with anything like this consistency.

- Although **thou** is the intimate pronoun, it is not standard between husband and wife; it is used only to express special affection or, as with any speakers, in anger or argument. Husbands use it more than wives do, and this use may be patronizing as well as affectionate.

- **Thou** is often used by parents to children, but not invariably. Again, it is reserved for special affection. It is virtually never used even by adult children to their parents. Parents use it less to their adult children, but we find mothers using **thou** to their adult sons when they want to exercise control over them (Gertrude to Hamlet, for example, and Volumnia to Coriolanus).

- **Thou** is the emotional pronoun: it is used to express anger, love, fear or grief. These powerful emotions may override considerations of social status or power relations, as we shall see in some of the scenes explored later.

- **Thou** use intensifies in the emotional 'hot spots' of the plays. We find it in love scenes, of course, and increasingly towards the end of tragedies and in scenes of comic confusion like the climax of *The Comedy of Errors*.

- Excessive, indiscriminate or inappropriate use of **thou** often goes along with a general loss of self-control. We find this in the language both of King Lear and of Timon in *Timon of Athens* as they descend into madness.

- A switch from **you** to **thou** or vice versa can be used to suggest that a character is adopting a new persona, either literally as in the case of Feste in *Twelfth Night* when he adopts the role of Sir Topaz the curate, or more subtly, as in the manipulative psychological games that Petruchio plays with Katherine, switching to **thou** when he is playing the wooer or pretending to be the concerned husband.

- **Thou** is also the rhetorical pronoun. It is used for 'speech acts' such as blessing, 'charging' and pleading; it is used for addressing anyone who is absent, sleeping or dead, and for addressing abstract entities like Fate or Love.

- Finally, although there are clear conventions about the use of **you** or **thou,** there are few rigid rules about the 'right' pronoun to use: one or the other may be the conventional or expected one in a given context, but it is always possible to use the unexpected one, so that the contrast with the expected produces an effect. Context is everything.

This theoretical framework is a necessary starting point but no-one is expected to take it all in at one reading. The workshop exercises and activities that follow are designed to flesh it out and take you, step by step, beyond the theoretical. Understanding the **you/thou** distinction intellectually takes you only so far; these exercises will take you to the point where you *feel* the difference instinctively and respond to it both physically and emotionally.

2

Practical sessions

Session one: Best friends

Texts: *As You Like It* Act 1 Scene 2 (Rosalind and Celia)
As You Like It Act 3 Scene 2 (Rosalind and Celia)
The Merchant of Venice Act 2 Scene 2 (Bassanio and Gratiano)

This session introduces the distance and closeness aspects of the **you/ thou** distinction by exploring how it works between close friends. There are two things in particular to notice here:

1   Because the choice of **you** or **thou** was so flexible, a switch can express or reflect a momentary change of attitude.

2   Asymmetry in the use of **thou,** where one speaker uses it more than the other, or where address with **thou** is met with a **you** reply – or vice versa – can reveal a good deal about the power dynamic of a relationship or suggest fissures beneath the surface.

Exercise 1: Mind the gap

In the text below, **thou** forms have been italicized to make the pronoun patterns clearer. You may find it helpful to use highlighter pens to mark the two sets of pronouns (pink for **thou** forms and blue for **you** forms work well, as **thou** is the warmer pronoun, **you** the cooler.) In pairs, walk through this exchange, taking one step forward for every **thou** form and one step back for every **you** form.

As You Like It Act 1 Scene 2, 1–23 (abridged text).
(*The scene takes place at court. Celia's father has just seized the throne from his elder brother, Rosalind's father, who has gone into exile.*)

CELIA

I pray *thee* Rosalind, sweet my coz, be merry.

ROSALIND

Dear Celia, I show more mirth than I am mistress of, and would **you** yet I were merrier?

[…]

CELIA

Herein I see *thou* lov'st me not with the full weight that I love *thee*. If my uncle, *thy* banished father, had banished *thy* uncle, the Duke my father, so *thou* hadst been with me, I could have taught my love to take *thy* father for mine. So wouldst *thou* if the truth of *thy* love to me were as righteously tempered as mine is to *thee*.

ROSALIND

Well, I will forget the condition of my estate to rejoice in **yours**.

CELIA

You know my father hath no child but I, nor none is like to have; and truly, when he dies, *thou* shalt be his heir, for what he hath taken away from *thy* father perforce I will render *thee* again in affection. By mine honour I will, and when I break that oath, let me turn monster. Therefore my sweet Rose, my dear Rose, be merry.

ROSALIND

From henceforth I will, coz, and devise sports. Let me see, what think **you** of falling in love?

Now, as a group, discuss the implications of this closeness and distance exercise:

- What is revealed about this close, cousinly friendship at this stage?
- What are the strains on the relationship?

Now consult the **Commentary** section near the back of the book (p. 77) for more suggestions and some answers.

Walk the exchange again, in pairs, freely (without the step forward/back constraints) but bearing in mind your findings from the step forward/back exercise.

Exercise 2: Mind the gap

Walk through this further scene between Rosalind and Celia, applying the step forward/back approach.

As You Like It Act 3 Scene 2, 176–223.
(Rosalind and Celia have fled to the forest of Arden to try to join Rosalind's father and his companions, who are living in exile there. Before they left the court, they met Orlando, whose father was loyal to Rosalind's father. For their safety, now they are in the Forest, Rosalind is dressed as a man, calling herself Ganymede, and they are posing as brother and sister. They have just discovered love poems to Rosalind hanging from the forest trees.)

CELIA

Trow **you** who hath done this?

ROSALIND

Is it a man?

CELIA

And a chain that **you** once wore about his neck. Change **you** colour?

ROSALIND

I *prithee* who?

CELIA

O Lord, Lord, it is a hard matter for friends to meet, but mountains may be removed with earthquakes, and so encounter.

ROSALIND

Nay but who is it?

CELIA

Is it possible?

ROSALIND

Nay, I *prithee* now with the most petitionary vehemence, tell me who it is.

CELIA

O wonderful, wonderful, and most wonderful, wonderful, and yet again wonderful, and after that out of all whooping!

ROSALIND

Good my complexion! Dost *thou* think because I am caparisoned like a man I have a doublet and hose in my disposition? One inch of delay more is a South Sea of discovery. I *prithee* tell me who is it quickly, and speak apace. I would *thou* couldst stammer, that *thou* might'st pour the concealed man out of *thy* mouth, as wine comes out of a narrow-mouthed bottle, either too much at once or none at all. I *prithee* take the cork out of *thy* mouth that I may drink *thy* tidings.

CELIA

So **you** may put a man in **your** belly.

ROSALIND

Is he of God's making? What manner of man? Is his head worth a hat? Or his chin worth a beard?

CELIA

Nay he hath but a little beard.

ROSALIND

Why, God will send more if the man will be thankful. Let me stay the growth of his beard if *thou* delay me not the knowledge of his chin.

CELIA

It is young Orlando, that tripped up the wrestler's heels and **your** heart both in an instant.

ROSALIND

Nay, but the devil take mocking! Speak sad brow and true maid.

CELIA

I'faith, coz, 'tis he.

ROSALIND

Orlando?

CELIA

Orlando.

ROSALIND

Alas the day! What shall I do with my doublet and hose? What did he when ***thou*** saw'st him? What said he? How looked he? Wherein went he? What makes he here? Did he ask for me? Where remains he? How parted he with ***thee*** and when shalt ***thou*** see him again? Answer me in one word.

CELIA

You must borrow me Gargantua's mouth first. 'Tis a word too great for any mouth of this age's size!

Discussion

- How has the **you/thou** pattern changed in this exchange?
- What possible reasons can you find for the changes?

Consult the **Commentary** (p. 79) and then walk through the scene freely (without the step forward/back constraints), bearing in mind your discussion.

Exercise 3: Mind the gap

Walk through this scene from *The Merchant of Venice* below.

The Merchant of Venice Act 2 Scene 2, 166–95.
(Bassanio and Gratiano are friends, members of a group of young men who enjoy good living and spending money. Bassanio is about to set out for Belmont, to woo Portia, a rich heiress.)

GRATIANO

Signior Bassanio!

BASSANIO Gratiano!

GRATIANO

I have a suit to **you**.

BASSANIO **You** have obtain'd it.

GRATIANO

You must not deny me, I must go with **you** to Belmont.

BASSANIO

Why then **you** must – but hear **thee** Gratiano,
Thou art too wild, too rude and bold of voice,
Parts that become **thee** happily enough,
And in such eyes as ours appear not faults –
But where **thou** art not known – why there they show
Something too liberal – pray **thee** take pains
To allay with some cold drops of modesty
Thy skipping spirit, lest through **thy** wild behaviour
I be misconst'red in the place I go to,
And lose my hopes.

GRATIANO Signior Bassanio, hear me –
If I do not put on a sober habit,
Talk with respect, and swear but now and then,
Wear prayer books in my pocket, look demurely,
Nay more, while grace is saying hood mine eyes
Thus with my hat, and sigh and say 'Amen':
Use all the observance of civility
Like one well studied in a sad ostent
To please his grandam, never trust me more.

BASSANIO

Well, we shall see **your** bearing.

GRATIANO

> Nay but I bar tonight, **you** shall not gauge me
> By what we do tonight.

BASSANIO   No that were pity,

> I would entreat **you** rather to put on
> **Your** boldest suit of mirth, for we have friends
> That purpose merriment; but fare **you** well,
> I have some business.

Discuss the following points:

- Why does Bassanio start using **thou** to Gratiano when he is telling him how to behave?
- How would that speech feel different if Bassanio used **you**?
- Why does he switch back into using **you** afterwards?
- Which pronoun do you think they usually use to each other?

Consult the **Commentary** on this text (p. 81) and then walk it through again, using the suggestions there.

Session two: Too wise to woo peaceably

Texts: *Much Ado About Nothing* Act 4 Scene 1 (Beatrice and Benedick)

Much Ado About Nothing Act 5 Scene 2 (Beatrice and Benedick)

The Taming of the Shrew Act 2 Scene 1 (Katherina and Petruchio)

This session looks at the ways **you** and **thou** can be used between lovers – in particular between combative lovers. Romeo and Juliet exemplify the convention that **thou** is the lovers' pronoun, using it consistently to one another throughout the play, but no other lovers in the plays do this, because conflicts and misunderstandings disturb their relationships. In the scenes below, the nearness and distance dynamic works again, but here we can see them as producing a 'courtship dance' as the man woos the woman.

- Look out again for sudden switches of pronoun and for asymmetry between the speakers.

Exercise 1: The courtship dance

In the scene below, use the step forward/back idea, but modify it: each **you** need not be accompanied by a step back – the actor can simply stay still – but **thou** should bring the actors closer together as the wooer expresses his love. The pronoun variations are in Benedick's speeches, so the movement variation will come from him too.

Much Ado About Nothing Act 4 Scene 1, 254–334 (abridged text).
(In the early part of the play, Beatrice and Benedick have constantly sparred with one another, and there is a hint that Beatrice once believed

that Benedick loved her but she was let down by him. Now their friends
have played a joke on them by convincing each of them that the other is
in love with them. The exchange below takes place in a church, where
there has just been a dramatic scene: Beatrice's cousin, Hero, was about
to marry Benedick's friend, Claudio, but Claudio has publicly spurned
her, believing that she has been unfaithful to him.)

Exeunt all but BENEDICK *and* BEATRICE

BENEDICK

Lady Beatrice, have **you** wept all this while?

BEATRICE

Yea, and I will weep a while longer.

BENEDICK

I will not desire that.

BEATRICE

You have no reason, I do it freely.

BENEDICK

Surely I do believe **your** fair cousin is wronged.

BEATRICE

Ah, how much might the man deserve of me that would right
her!

BENEDICK

Is there any way to show such friendship?

BEATRICE

A very even way, but no such friend.

BENEDICK

May a man do it?

BEATRICE

It is a man's office, but not **yours**.

BENEDICK

I do love nothing in the world so well as **you** – is not that strange?

BEATRICE

As strange as the thing I know not. It were as possible for me to say I loved nothing so well as **you**, but believe me not, I confess nothing, nor I deny nothing. I am sorry for my cousin.

BENEDICK

By my sword, Beatrice, **thou** lovest me.

BEATRICE

Do not swear and eat it.

BENEDICK

I will swear by it that **you** love me, and will make him eat it that swears I love not **you**.

BEATRICE

Will **you** not eat **your** word?

BENEDICK

With no sauce that can be devised to it. I protest I love **thee**.

BEATRICE

Why then, God forgive me!

BENEDICK

What offence, sweet Beatrice?

BEATRICE

You have stayed me in a happy hour, I was about to protest I loved **you**.

BENEDICK

And do it with all **thy** heart.

BEATRICE

I love **you** with so much of my heart that none is left to protest.

BENEDICK

Come, bid me do anything for **thee**.

BEATRICE

Kill Claudio!

BENEDICK

Ha, not for the wide world!

BEATRICE

You kill me to deny it. Farewell.

BENEDICK

Tarry, sweet Beatrice.

BEATRICE

I am gone, though I am here; there is no love in **you**; nay I pray **you** let me go.

BENEDICK

Beatrice –

BEATRICE

In faith, I will go.

BENEDICK

We'll be friends first.

BEATRICE

You dare easier be friends with me than fight with mine enemy.

BENEDICK

Is Claudio **thine** enemy?

BEATRICE

Is he not approved in the height a villain, that hath slandered, scorned, dishonoured my kinswoman? O that I were a man! What, bear her in hand until they come to take hands, and then with public accusation, uncovered slander, unmitigated rancour – O God that I were a man! I would eat his heart in the market-place.

BENEDICK

Hear me, Beatrice.

BEATRICE

Talk with a man out at a window! A proper saying!

BENEDICK

Nay, but Beatrice –

BEATRICE

Sweet Hero! She is wronged, she is slandered, she is undone.

[...]

BENEDICK

Tarry, good Beatrice. By this hand I love **thee**.

BEATRICE

Use it for my love some other way than swearing by it.

BENEDICK

Think **you** in **your** soul the Count Claudio hath wronged Hero?

BEATRICE

Yea, as sure as I have a thought, or a soul.

BENEDICK

Enough! I am engaged, I will challenge him. I will kiss **your** hand, and so I leave **you**. By this hand Claudio shall render me a dear account. Go comfort **your** cousin; I must say she is dead; and so farewell.

Exeunt

Discussion

- Neither Benedick nor Beatrice has used **thou** to the other previously. Why does Benedick do so now?

- Why do you think Beatrice does not use **thou** in return (especially when she says 'I love **you**', which is very unusual?)

- What specific reasons can you find for Benedick's switches between **you** and **thou**?

Now consult the **Commentary** on this scene (p. 84) and walk it through freely, bearing the ideas there, and your discussion, in mind.

Exercise 2: The courtship dance

Look at the text below and take the same approach as you did with the one above (the modified step forward/back approach).

Much Ado About Nothing Act 5 Scene 2, 42–97 (abridged text). *(Benedick has taken up Beatrice's command to kill Claudio and has challenged him to a duel.)*

Enter BEATRICE

BENEDICK

Sweet Beatrice, wouldst **thou** come when I called **thee**?

BEATRICE

Yea, signor, and depart when **you** bid me.

BENEDICK

O, stay but till then.

BEATRICE

'Then' is spoken: fare **you** well now. And yet ere I go, let me go with that I came, which is, with knowing what hath passed between **you** and Claudio.

BENEDICK

Only foul words – and thereupon I will kiss **thee**.

BEATRICE

Foul words is but foul wind, and foul wind is but foul breath and foul breath is noisome, therefore I will depart unkissed.

BENEDICK

Thou has frighted the word out of his right sense, so forcible is **thy** wit. But I must tell **thee** plainly, Claudio undergoes my challenge, and either I must shortly hear from him, or I will subscribe him a coward. And I pray **thee** now tell me, for which of my bad parts didst **thou** first fall in love with me?

BEATRICE

For them all together, which maintained so politic a state of evil that they will not admit any good part to intermingle with them. But for which of my good parts did **you** first suffer love for me?

BENEDICK

'Suffer love' – a good epithet! I do suffer love indeed, for I love **thee** against my will.

BEATRICE

In spite of **your** heart, I think. Alas, poor heart! If **you** will spite it for my sake, I will spite it for **yours**, for I will never love that which my friend hates.

BENEDICK

Thou and I are too wise to woo peaceably.

BEATRICE

It appears not in this confession: there's not one wise man among twenty that will praise himself.

[…]

BENEDICK

So much for praising myself, who I myself will bear witness is praiseworthy. And now tell me, how doth **your** cousin?

BEATRICE

Very ill.

BENEDICK

And how do **you**?

BEATRICE

Very ill too.

BENEDICK

Serve God, love me, and mend. There will I leave **you** too, for here comes one in haste.

Enter URSULA

URSULA

Madam, **you** must come to **your** uncle – yonder's old coil at home. It is proved my Lady Hero hath been falsely accused, the

Prince and Claudio mightily abused, and Don John is the author of all, who is fled and gone. Will **you** come presently?

BEATRICE

Will **you** go hear this news signior?

BENEDICK

I will live in **thy** heart, die in **thy** lap and be buried in **thy** eyes: and moreover, I will go with **thee** to **thy** uncle's.

Exeunt

Discussion

- What change, if any, do you notice in Benedick's use of **thou**? How do you explain that?

- Why do you think he switches to **you** when he asks about Hero?

- What reasons can you suggest for Beatrice continuing to use **you** to Benedick?

- What character indicators does her consistent use of **you** offer to an actor?

Now consult the **Commentary** (p. 88)

Exercise 3: The courtship dance

Take the modified step forward/back approach to this extract from *The Taming of the Shrew*.

The Taming of the Shrew Act 2 Scene 1, 183–274.
(Katherina has a reputation for being 'shrewish' and has no suitors; Petruchio has arrived in Padua looking for a rich wife. Eager to get Katherina married off, her father has agreed that Petruchio will marry her, although the couple have never met.)

Enter KATHERINA

PETRUCHIO

Good morrow Kate, for that's **your** name, I hear.

KATHERINA

Well have **you** heard, but something hard of hearing;
They call me Katherine that do talk of me.

PETRUCHIO

You lie, in faith, for **you** are call'd plain Kate,
And bonny Kate and sometimes Kate the curst;
But Kate, the prettiest Kate in Christendom,
Kate of Kate Hall, my super-dainty Kate,
For dainties are all Kates, and therefore, Kate,
Take this of me, Kate of my consolation,
Hearing **thy** mildness prais'd in every town,
Thy virtues spoke of, and **thy** beauty sounded,
Yet not so deeply as to **thee** belongs,
Myself am mov'd to woo **thee** for my wife.

KATHERINA

Mov'd in good time! Let him that mov'd **you** hither
Remove **you** hence. I knew **you** at the first
You were a movable.

PETRUCHIO   Why, what's a movable?

KATHERINA

A joint stool.

PETRUCHIO   **Thou** hast hit it. Come, sit on me.

KATHERINA

Asses are made to bear, and so are **you**.

PETRUCHIO

Women are made to bear, and so are **you**.

KATHERINA

No such jade as **you**, if me **you** mean.

PETRUCHIO

Alas, good Kate, I will not burden **thee**!
For knowing **thee** to be but young and light –

KATHERINA

Too light for such a swain as **you** to catch,
And yet as heavy as my weight should be.

PETRUCHIO

Should be? Should – buzz!

KATHERINA   Well ta'en, and like a buzzard.

PETRUCHIO

O slow-wing'd turtle, shall a buzzard take **thee**?

KATHERINA

Ay, for a turtle, as he takes a buzzard.

PETRUCHIO

Come, come **you** wasp; i'faith, **you** are too angry.

KATHERINA

If I be waspish, best beware my sting.

PETRUCHIO

My remedy is then to pluck it out.

KATHERINA

Ay, if the fool could find where it lies.

PETRUCHIO

Who knows not where a wasp does wear his sting?
In his tail.

KATHERINA

In his tongue.

PETRUCHIO   Whose tongue?

KATHERINA

Yours, if **you** talk of tales, and so farewell.

PETRUCHIO

What, with my tongue in **your** tail? Nay, come again,
Good Kate. I am a gentleman –

KATHERINA   That I'll try.

She strikes him

PETRUCHIO

I swear I'll cuff **you**, if **you** strike again.

KATHERINA

So may **you** lose **your** arms.
If **you** strike me, **you** are no gentleman,
And if no gentleman, why then no arms.

PETRUCHIO

A herald, Kate? O, put me in **thy** books.

KATHERINA

What is **your** crest, a coxcomb?

PETRUCHIO

A combless cock, so Kate will be my hen.

KATHERINA

No cock of mine, **you** crow too like a craven.

PETRUCHIO

Nay, come, Kate, come; **you** must not look so sour.

KATHERINA

It is my fashion when I see a crab.

PETRUCHIO

Why, here's no crab, and therefore look not sour.

KATHERINA

There is, there is.

PETRUCHIO

Then show it me.

KATHERINA

Had I a glass, I would.

PETRUCHIO

What, **you** mean my face?

KATHERINA

Well aim'd of such a young one.

PETRUCHIO

Now, by Saint George, I am too young for **you**.

KATHERINA

Yet **you** are wither'd.

PETRUCHIO   'Tis with cares.

KATHERINA   I care not.

PETRUCHIO

> Nay, hear **you** Kate – in sooth, **you** scape not so.

KATHERINA

> I chafe **you**, if I tarry. Let me go.

PETRUCHIO

> No, not a whit. I find **you** passing gentle.
> 'Twas told me **you** were rough, and coy, and sullen,
> And now I find report a very liar;
> For **thou** art pleasant, gamesome, passing courteous,
> But slow in speech, yet sweet as springtime flowers.
> **Thou** canst not frown, **thou** canst not look askance,
> Nor bite the lip, as angry wenches will,
> Nor hast **thou** pleasure to be cross in talk.
> But **thou** with mildness entertain'st **thy** wooers,
> With gentle conference, soft and affable.
> Why does the world report that Kate doth limp?
> O slanderous world! Kate like the hazel-twig
> Is straight and slender, and as brown in hue
> As hazel-nuts and sweeter than the kernels.
> O, let me see **thee** walk. **Thou** dost not halt.

KATHERINA

> Go, fool, and whom **thou** keep'st command.

PETRUCHIO

> Did ever Dian so become a grove
> As Kate this chamber with her princely gait?
> O be **thou** Dian, and let her be Kate,
> And then let Kate be chaste and Dian sportful.

KATHERINA

> Where did **you** study all this goodly speech?

PETRUCHIO

It is extempore, from my mother-wit.

KATHERINA

A witty mother, witless else her son.

PETRUCHIO

Am I not wise?

KATHERINA   Yes, keep **you** warm.

PETRUCHIO

Marry, so I mean, sweet Katherine, in **thy** bed.
And therefore, setting all this chat aside,
Thus in plain terms; **your** father hath consented
That **you** shall be my wife; **your** dowry 'greed on:
And will **you**, nill **you**, I will marry **you**.
Now Kate, I am a husband for **your** turn,
For by this light, whereby I see **thy** beauty,
Thy beauty that doth make me like **thee** well,
Thou must be married to no man but me.
For I am he am born to tame **you**, Kate,
And bring **you** from a wild Kate to a Kate
Conformable as other household Kates.
Here comes **your** father. Never make denial.
I must and will have Katherine for my wife.

Discussion

- Petruchio uses **thou** to Katherina very early in the scene.
  What does this suggest about his character and his attitude
  towards marrying her?

- Towards the end of their conversation, when he is telling her
  that he will marry her, Petruchio switches to and fro between
  thou and **you**. How do you explain the switches?

- Katherina uses **thou** only once in this scene. She is very angry with Petruchio and **thou** is often used to express anger and contempt. Why do you think she does not use **thou** more?

After consulting the notes on this scene in the **Commentary** (p. 91), walk it through again.

Session three: Unwelcome advances

Texts: *As You Like It* Act 3 Scene 5 (Silvius and Phebe)
The Two Gentlemen of Verona Act 5 Scene 4 (Proteus and Silvia)

This session looks at what happens when would-be lovers know that they are not welcome. In the previous session we saw how Petruchio behaves as though he is a welcome wooer to Katherina, even though they have never met before and he knows her reputation as a difficult woman. This is unusual – unwelcome wooers are usually more cautious.

Exercise 1: Which pronoun?

Below are four alternative versions of dialogue between Silvius and Phebe in *As You Like It*. Each of them, in the original text, uses only one pronoun throughout, but which one? Do they both use the same pronoun or different ones?

As You Like It Act 3 Scene 5, 1–34.
Version 1

Enter PHEBE and SILVIUS

SILVIUS

Sweet Phebe, do not scorn me, do not, Phebe.
Say that **you** love me not but say not so
In bitterness. The common executioner,
Whose heart th'accustomed sight of death makes hard,
Falls not the axe upon the humbled neck
But first begs pardon. Will **you** sterner be
Than he that dies and lives by bloody drops?

PHEBE

    I would not be **your** executioner.

    I fly **you** for I would not injure **you**.

    You tell me there is murder in mine eye:

    'Tis pretty, sure, and very probable

    That eyes, that are the frail'st and softest things,

    That shut their coward gates on atomies,

    Should be call'd tyrants, butchers, murderers!

    Now I do frown on **you** with all my heart

    And if mine eyes can wound now let them kill **you**.

    Now counterfeit to swoon, why now fall down,–

    Or if **you** can not, O for shame, for shame,

    Lie not to say mine eyes are murderers!

    Now show the wound mine eye hath made in **you**.

    Scratch **you** but with a pin and there remains

    Some scar of it. Lean but upon a rush,

    The cicatrice and capable impressure

    Your palm some moment keeps; but now mine eyes

    Which I have darted at **you** hurt **you** not,

    Nor, I am sure, there is no power in eyes

    That can do hurt.

SILVIUS   O dear Phebe,

    If ever, as that ever may be near,

    You find in some fresh cheek the power of fancy,

    Then shall **you** see the wounds invisible

    That love's keen arrow makes.

PHEBE   But till that time

    Come not near me, and when that time comes

    Afflict me with **your** mocks, pity me not,

    As till that time I shall not pity **you**.

Version 2

SILVIUS

Sweet Phebe, do not scorn me, do not, Phebe.

Say that **thou** lov'st me not but say not so

In bitterness. The common executioner,

Whose heart th'accustomed sight of death makes hard,

Falls not the axe upon the humbled neck

But first begs pardon. Wilt **thou** sterner be

Than he that dies and lives by bloody drops?

PHEBE

I would not be **thy** executioner.

I fly **thee** for I would not injure **thee**.

Thou tell'st me there is murder in mine eye:

'Tis pretty, sure, and very probable

That eyes, that are the frail'st and softest things,

That shut their coward gates on atomies,

Should be call'd tyrants, butchers, murderers!.

Now I do frown on **thee** with all my heart

And if mine eyes can wound now let them kill **thee**.

Now counterfeit to swoon, why now fall down,–

Or if **thou** canst not, O for shame, for shame,

Lie not to say mine eyes are murderers!

Now show the wound mine eye hath made in **thee**.

Scratch **thee** but with a pin and there remains

Some scar of it. Lean but upon a rush,

The cicatrice and capable impressure

Thy palm some moment keeps; but now mine eyes

Which I have darted at **thee** hurt **thee** not,

Nor, I am sure, there is no power in eyes

That can do hurt.

SILVIUS   O dear Phebe,
　　If ever, as that ever may be near,
　　Thou find'st in some fresh cheek the power of fancy,
　　Then shalt **thou** see the wounds invisible
　　That love's keen arrow makes.

PHEBE　　　　　　　　　　　　But till that time
　　Come not near me, and when that time comes
　　Afflict me with **thy** mocks, pity me not,
　　As till that time I shall not pity **thee**.

Version 3

SILVIUS
　　Sweet Phebe, do not scorn me, do not, Phebe.
　　Say that **thou** lov'st me not but say not so
　　In bitterness. The common executioner,
　　Whose heart th'accustomed sight of death makes hard,
　　Falls not the axe upon the humbled neck
　　But first begs pardon. Wilt **thou** sterner be
　　Than he that dies and lives by bloody drops?

PHEBE
　　I would not be **your** executioner.
　　I fly **you** for I would not injure **you**.
　　You tell me there is murder in mine eye:
　　'Tis pretty, sure, and very probable
　　That eyes, that are the frail'st and softest things,
　　That shut their coward gates on atomies,
　　Should be call'd tyrants, butchers, murderers!.
　　Now I do frown on **you** with all my heart
　　And if mine eyes can wound now let them kill **you**.
　　Now counterfeit to swoon, why now fall down,–

Or if **you** can not, O for shame, for shame,
Lie not to say mine eyes are murderers!
Now show the wound mine eye hath made in **you**.
Scratch **you** but with a pin and there remains
Some scar of it. Lean but upon a rush,
The cicatrice and capable impressure
Your palm some moment keeps; but now mine eyes
Which I have darted at **you** hurt **you** not,
Nor, I am sure, there is no power in eyes
That can do hurt.

SILVIUS   O dear Phebe,
If ever, as that ever may be near,
Thou find'st in some fresh cheek the power of fancy,
Then shalt **thou** see the wounds invisible
That love's keen arrow makes.

PHEBE   But till that time
Come not near me, and when that time comes
Afflict me with **your** mocks, pity me not,
As till that time I shall not pity **you**.

Version 4

SILVIUS
Sweet Phebe, do not scorn me, do not, Phebe.
Say that **you** love me not but say not so
In bitterness. The common executioner,
Whose heart th'accustomed sight of death makes hard,
Falls not the axe upon the humbled neck
But first begs pardon. Will **you** sterner be
Than he that dies and lives by bloody drops?

PHEBE

I would not be **thy** executioner.

I fly **thee** for I would not injure **thee**.

Thou tell'st me there is murder in mine eye:

'Tis pretty, sure, and very probable

That eyes, that are the frail'st and softest things,

That shut their coward gates on atomies,

Should be call'd tyrants, butchers, murderers!.

Now I do frown on **thee** with all my heart

And if mine eyes can wound now let them kill **thee**.

Now counterfeit to swoon, why now fall down,–

Or if **thou** canst not, O for shame, for shame,

Lie not to say mine eyes are murderers!

Now show the wound mine eye hath made in **thee**.

Scratch **thee** but with a pin and there remains

Some scar of it. Lean but upon a rush,

The cicatrice and capable impressure

Thy palm some moment keeps; but now mine eyes

Which I have darted at **thee** hurt **thee** not,

Nor, I am sure, there is no power in eyes

That can do hurt.

SILVIUS   O dear Phebe,

If ever, as that ever may be near,

You find in some fresh cheek the power of fancy,

Then shall **you** see the wounds invisible

That love's keen arrow makes.

PHEBE   But till that time

Come not near me, and when that time comes

Afflict me with **thy** mocks, pity me not,

As till that time I shall not pity **thee**.

- Try acting each version in turn.

- Discuss what the effect is of the pronouns in each one. Bear in mind the three main uses of **thou**; for social condescension, for affection and intimacy and for anger or contempt. Then decide which of the versions is Shakespeare's text.

- Now consult the **Commentary** (p. 99), try the correct version again and see what effects you can achieve.

Exercise 2: Which pronoun?

In the original version of the text below, Silvia uses **thou** consistently to Proteus but he uses **thee** just once to her. In this text **thee** has been replaced by **you**. Read through the scene and discuss:

- Why Silvia uses **thou** to Valentine, her unwelcome wooer.

- Where Proteus's switch to **thee** might happen, bearing in mind the physical closeness that is often associated with **thou/ thee**. Walk through your alternative suggestions before consulting the **Commentary** (p. 99).

The Two Gentlemen of Verona Act 5 Scene 4, 19–59.
(Silvia and her lover Valentine were planning to elope but Proteus, Valentine's best friend, who is also in love with Silvia, has told her father, the Duke of Milan, of their plans and Valentine has been banished. Silvia, travelling alone to find Valentine, has been seized by outlaws and then rescued by Proteus, who is in pursuit of her.)

Enter PROTEUS and SILVIA

PROTEUS
    Madam, this service I have done for **you**
    (Though **you** respect not aught **your** servant doth)
    To hazard life, and rescue **you** from him
    That would have forc'd **your** honour and **your** love.

Vouchsafe me for my meed but one fair look.

A smaller boon than this I cannot beg,

And less than this I am sure **you** cannot give.

SILVIA

O miserable, unhappy that I am!

PROTEUS

Unhappy were **you** madam, ere I came;

But by my coming I have made **you** happy.

SILVIA

By **thy** approach **thou** mak'st me most unhappy.

Had I been seized by a hungry lion,

I would have been a breakfast to the beast,

Rather than have false Proteus rescue me.

O heaven be judge how I love Valentine,

Whose life's as tender to me as my soul,

And full as much (for more there cannot be)

I do detest false perjur'd Proteus:

Therefore be gone, solicit me no more.

PROTEUS

What dangerous action, stood it next to death,

Would I not undergo for one calm look?

O 'tis the curse in love and still approved,

When women cannot love where they're belov'd.

SILVIA

When Proteus cannot love where he's belov'd.

Read over Julia's heart, **thy** first best love,

For whose dear sake **thou** didst then rend **thy** faith

Into a thousand oaths; and all those oaths

Descended into perjury, to love me.

Thou hast no faith left now, unless **thou**'dst two,
And that's far worse than none: better have none
Than plural faith, which is too much by one.
Thou counterfeit to **thy** true friend!

PROTEUS

In love, who respects friend?

SILVIA   All men but Proteus.

PROTEUS

Nay, if the gentle spirit of moving words
Can no way change **you** to a milder form,
I'll woo **you** like a soldier, at arms end,
And love **you** 'gainst the nature of love: force **you**.

SILVIA

O heaven!

PROTEUS   I'll force **you** yield to my desire.

VALENTINE *(coming forward)*
Ruffian! Let go that rude uncivil touch,
Thou friend of an ill fashion!

Consult the **Commentary** (p. 101). Did you identify the change of pronoun? How might that affect Proteus's actions?

Session four: Lèse-majesté

Texts: *The Winter's Tale* Act 2 Scene 3 (Paulina to Leontes)
             The Winter's Tale Act 3 Scene 2 (Paulina to Leontes)
             King Lear Act 1 Scene 1 (Kent to Lear)
             Measure for Measure Act 2 Scene 4 (Isabella to Angelo)

It is unusual for anyone to address a king or other ruler with **thou** because the social convention requires the respectful pronoun and very few people are on intimate terms with the king (after Macbeth becomes king, Lady Macbeth never again uses **thou** to him). However, there are highly dramatic moments when a character is so moved by anger that they disregard the consequences of speaking disrespectfully, and they recklessly use **thou.** An interesting example is in *Richard III*, where all the men use **you** to Richard, with a lot of respectful honorific titles like 'my lord', 'sire', '**your** majesty', while all the women **thou** him, and spit insulting epithets at him ('bottled spider', 'toad' and so on). They have reached a point where they have already suffered so much at Richard's hands – losing their husbands and their children – that they no longer care about the consequences.

The situation has to be extreme for someone to **thou** a king, and the **thou**ing itself is a marker of the desperation a character is feeling.

Exercise 1: Why the change?

We look first at Paulina in *The Winter's Tale*. Look at the two scenes below, act them out and consider:

- What motivates Paulina's switch to **thou** in the second scene.
- How Paulina's second speech feels different in intensity from her first and how this would affect the movement and staging of the scenes.

The Winter's Tale Act 2 Scene 3, 113–29 (abridged text).

(King Leontes has conceived a sudden and irrational belief that his wife has had an affair with his oldest friend. He has had her thrown into prison, where she has given birth to a baby daughter. Leontes denies that the child is his but Paulina, the queen's lady-in-waiting, has brought the baby to him in the hope of softening his heart. He, however, has flown into a rage.)

LEONTES

    I'll have **thee** burnt!

PAULINA   I care not

    It is an heretic that makes the fire,

    Not she that burns in't. I'll not call **you** tyrant;

    But this most cruel usage of **your** queen –

    Not able to produce more accusation

    Than **your** own weak-hing'd fancy – something savours

    Of tyranny and will ignoble make **you**,

    Yea, scandalous to the world.

LEONTES   On **your** allegiance,

    Out of the chamber with her!

    […]

                 Away with her!

PAULINA

    I pray **you** do not push me; I'll be gone.

    Look to **your** babe, my lord: 'tis **yours**. Jove send her

    A better guiding spirit!

    So, so: farewell; we are gone.

Exit

The Winter's Tale Act 3 Scene 2, 173–99.

(Hermione, the queen, has been put on trial by Leontes. At the end of the trial, news has come that Mamilius, their son, is dead, Hermione has collapsed, and has been carried off to be cared for by Paulina.)

Enter PAULINA

PAULINA

> What studied torments, tyrant, hast for me?
> What wheels, racks, fires? What flaying, boiling
> In leads or oils? What old or newer torture
> Must I receive, whose every word deserves
> To taste of **thy** most worse? **Thy** tyranny,
> Together working with **thy** jealousies
> (Fancies too weak for boys, too green and idle
> For girls of nine), O think what they have done,
> And then run mad indeed: stark mad! For all
> **Thy** bygone fooleries were but spices of it.
> That **thou** betray'dst Polixenes, 'twas nothing:
> That did but show **thee**, of a fool, inconstant
> And damnable ingrateful; nor was't much,
> **Thou** would'st have poison'd good Camillo's honour,
> To have him kill a king; poor trespasses,
> More monstrous standing by: whereof I reckon
> The casting forth to crows **thy** baby daughter
> To be none or little; though a devil
> Would have shed water out of fire, ere done't:
> Nor is't directly laid to **thee** the death
> Of the young prince, whose honourable thoughts
> (Thoughts high for one so tender) cleft the heart

> That could conceive a gross and foolish sire
> Blemish'd his gracious dam: this is not, no,
> Laid to **thy** answer: but the last – O lords,
> When I have said, cry 'woe!' – the queen, the queen,
> The sweetest, dearest creature's dead; and vengeance for't
> Not dropped down yet.

Now consult the **Commentary** (p. 105)

Exercise 2: Which pronoun?

The text below is from the opening scene of *King Lear*. This version of the text below has been doctored so that all the pronouns are **you**s. Try acting it out as it appears here.

King Lear Act 1 Scene 1, 145–90.
(Lear has announced, in front of the whole court, that he is going to abdicate and divide his kingdom of Britain into three parts, one for each of his three daughters. First, though, he has demanded that his daughters earn their shares by declaring how much they love him. His elder daughters, Goneril and Regan, have made insincere, flattering speeches, but Cordelia, his youngest and favourite daughter, has refused to speak, saying that she loves him but cannot 'heave her heart into her mouth'. In a rage, Lear has disowned her and declared that her share is to be divided between her sisters. The Earl of Kent, Lear's loyal councillor, attempts to intervene on Cordelia's behalf.)

KENT   Royal Lear,
> Whom I have ever honoured as my king,
> Loved as my father, as my master followed,
> As my great patron thought on in my prayers –

LEAR

The bow is bent and drawn; make from the shaft.

KENT

Let it fall rather, though the fork invade
The region of my heart: be Kent unmannerly
When Lear is mad. What would **you** do, old man?
Think **you** that duty shall have dread to speak,
When power to flattery bows? To plainness honour's bound
When majesty falls to folly. Reserve **your** state,
And in **your** best consideration check
This hideous rashness. Answer my life my judgement,
Your youngest daughter does not love **you** least,
Nor are those empty-hearted, whose low sounds
Reverb no hollowness.

LEAR   Kent, on **your** life, no more.

KENT

My life I never held but as a pawn
To wage against **your** enemies, ne'er fear to lose it,
Your safety being the motive.

LEAR   Out of my sight!

KENT

See better, Lear, and let me still remain
The true blank of **your** eye.

LEAR

Now by Apollo!

KENT   Now by Apollo, King,
You swear **your** gods in vain.

LEAR   O vassal! Miscreant!

KENT

> Do, kill **your** physician, and **your** fee bestow
> Upon the foul disease. Revoke **your** gift,
> Or whilst I can vent clamour from my throat
> I'll tell **you, you** do evil.

LEAR

> Hear me, recreant, on **your** allegiance, hear me:
> That **you** have sought to make us break our vows,
> Which we durst never yet, and with strained pride
> To come betwixt our sentence and our power,
> Which nor our nature, nor our place can bear,
> Our potency made good, take **your** reward.
> Five days do we allot **you** for provision,
> To shield **you** from disasters of the world,
> And on the sixth to turn **your** hated back
> Upon our kingdom. If on the next day following
> **Your** banished trunk be found in our dominions,
> The moment is **your** death. Away, By Jupiter,
> This shall not be revoked.

KENT

> Why, fare **you** well, King, since thus **you** will appear,
> Freedom lives hence and banishment is here.
> (*to* CORDELIA) The gods to their dear shelter take **you**, maid,
> That justly thinks and has most rightly said;
> (*to* GONERIL *and* REGAN) And **your** large speeches may **your**
>   deeds approve,
> That good effects may spring from words of love.
> Thus Kent, O Princes, bids **you** all adieu;
> He'll shape his old course in a country new.

Exit

- Try acting out this text as it stands.

- Look at the text and discuss where you think there are **thou** forms in the authentic text

- Go to the **Commentary** (p. 107) to find the authentic text.

- Act out the authentic version.

- Discussion: what is the impact of this version on actors and audience, compared with the doctored **you** version?

Exercise 3: Where's the switch?

The text below is taken from *Measure for Measure*. It has been doctored so that **thou**s have been replaced with **you**s. Walk it through and then discuss:

- Where Isabella might use **thou**
- Where Angelo might use **thou**

Measure for Measure Act 2 Scene 4, 140–69.
(Angelo has been appointed by the Duke of Vienna to govern the city in his absence. Angelo has declared it his mission to clean up moral corruption in the city and has sentenced Isabella's brother, Claudio, to be put to death for getting his fiancée, Juliet, pregnant. Isabella, a novice nun, has come to Angelo to beg for mercy for her brother. Angelo offers her a bargain: he will pardon her brother if she will sleep with him.)

ANGELO

Plainly conceive, I love **you**.

ISABELLA

My brother did love Juliet,
And **you** tell me that he shall die for't.

ANGELO

 He shall not, Isabel, if **you** give me love.

ISABELLA

 I know **your** virtue hath a licence in't
 Which seems a little fouler than it is,
 To pluck on others.

ANGELO   Believe me, on mine honour,
 My words express my purpose.

ISABELLA

 Ha? Little honour, to be much believ'd,
 And most pernicious purpose! Seeming, seeming!
 I will proclaim **you**, Angelo, look for't.
 Sign me a present pardon for my brother,
 Or with an outstretch'd throat I'll tell the world aloud
 What man **you** are.

ANGELO   Who will believe **you**, Isabel?
 My unsoil'd name, th'austereness of my life,
 My vouch against **you**, and my place i'th' state
 Will so **your** accusation overweigh,
 That **you** shall stifle in **your** own report,
 And smell of calumny. I have begun
 And now I give my sensual race the rein:
 Fit **your** consent to my sharp appetite;
 Lay by all nicety and prolixious blushes
 That banish what they sue for. Redeem **your** brother
 By yielding up **your** body to my will;
 Or else he must not only die the death,
 But **your** unkindness shall his death draw out
 To lingering sufferance. Answer me tomorrow,

> Or by the affection that now guides me most,
> I'll prove a tyrant to him. As for **you**,
> Say what **you** can: my false o'erweighs **your** true.

When you have decided where there might be **thou**s, consult the **Commentary** (p. 110) and look at the authentic version.

Act out the authentic version and discuss how the switches to **thou** help with the emotional temperature of the dialogue.

Session five: Family values

Texts: *Hamlet* Act 1 Scene 2 (Claudius, Gertrude, Hamlet, Laertes)
Hamlet Act 1 Scene 3 (Polonius, Laertes, Ophelia)

In this session, we look at two scenes from *Hamlet* to consider family relationships, particularly those between parents and adult children. The power dynamic between parents and children means that even adult sons and daughters do not use **thou** to their parents. Parents will use **thou** affectionately to young children and they may use **thou** to adult children, but it is unusual.

Exercise 1: Where do we go?

Look at the extract below and consider how it should be staged, then walk it through.

Hamlet Act 1 Scene 2, 42–120 (abridged text).
(Hamlet's father, the King of Denmark, has died while Hamlet was studying abroad. His uncle, Claudius, has seized the throne and has just married his brother's widow, Gertrude, Hamlet's mother. This scene is their first public appearance before the court as husband and wife. Polonius is the Lord Chamberlain; his son, Laertes, has also been studying abroad. King Claudius has just been dealing with ambassadors from Norway and now turns to Laertes.)

KING
    And now, Laertes, what's the news with **you**?
    You told us of some suit: what is't Laertes?
    You cannot speak of reason to the Dane
    And lose **your** voice. What wouldst **thou** beg, Laertes,
    That shall not be my offer, not **thy** asking?

The head is not more native to the heart,
The hand more instrumental to the mouth,
Than is the throne of Denmark to **thy** father.
What wouldst **thou** have Laertes?

LAERTES   My dread lord,
Your leave and favour to return to France,
From whence though willingly I came to Denmark
To show my duty in **your** coronation,
Yet now I must confess, that duty done,
My thoughts and wishes bend again toward France
And bow them to **your** gracious leave and pardon.

KING

Have **you your** father's leave? What says Polonius?

POLONIUS

He hath, my lord, wrung from me my slow leave
By laboursome petition, and at last
Upon his will I seal'd my hard consent.
I do beseech **you** give him leave to go.

KING

Take **thy** fair hour, Laertes, time be **thine**,
And **thy** best graces spend it at **thy** will.
But now, my cousin Hamlet, and my son –

HAMLET

A little more than kin, and less than kind.

KING

How is it that the clouds still hang on **you**?

HAMLET

Not so, my lord, I am too much in the sun

QUEEN

> Good Hamlet, cast **thy** nighted colour off,
> And let **thine** eye look like a friend on Denmark.
> Do not for ever with **thy** vailed lids
> Seek for **thy** noble father in the dust.
> **Thou** know'st 'tis common: all that lives, must die,
> Passing through nature to eternity.

HAMLET

> Ay, madam, it is common.

QUEEN   If it be,
> Why seems it so particular with **thee**?

HAMLET

> Seems, madam? Nay, it is. I know not 'seems'.
> 'Tis not alone my inky cloak, good mother,
> Nor customary suits of solemn black
> That can denote me truly. These indeed seem,
> But I have that within which passes show,
> These but the trappings and the suits of woe.

KING

> 'Tis sweet and commendable in **your** nature, Hamlet,
> To give these mourning duties to **your** father,
> But **you** must know **your** father lost a father,
> That father lost, lost his, and the survivor bound
> In filial obligation for some term
> To do obsequious sorrow. But to persever
> In obstinate condolement is a course
> Of impious stubbornness, 'tis unmanly grief.
> [...]
>   We pray **you** throw to earth

This unprevailing woe, and think of us
As of a father; for let the world take note
You are the most immediate to our throne,
And with no less nobility of love
Than that which dearest father bears his son
Do I impart toward **you**. For **your** intent
In going back to school in Wittenberg
It is most retrograde to our desire,
And we beseech **you** bend **you** to remain
Here in the cheer and comfort of our eye,
Our chiefest courtier, cousin and our son.

QUEEN

Let not **thy** mother lose her prayers, Hamlet.
I pray **thee** stay with us. Go not to Wittenberg.

HAMLET

I shall in all my best obey **you**, madam.

Discussion

- There are several contrasts in **you/thou** use here. What contrasts do you notice?
- Why do you think the King starts to use **thou** to Laertes?
- Why does the King not use **thou** to Hamlet, his nephew and stepson?
- What particular reasons might there be for Gertrude to use **thou** to Hamlet?

Turn to the **Commentary** (p. 113) and then act out the scene again if you feel there are changes you could make in staging and movement.

Exercise 2: Who's the favourite?

Hamlet Act 1 Scene 3, 55–136 (abridged text).
(Laertes is about to leave, to return to university in Paris. He has just been saying goodbye to his sister, Ophelia, when their father joins them.)

Enter POLONIUS

POLONIUS

Yet here, Laertes? Aboard, aboard for shame.
The wind sits in the shoulder of **your** sail
And **you** are stay'd for. There, my blessing with **thee**.
And these few precepts in **thy** memory
Look **thou** character. Give **thy** thoughts no tongue,
Nor any unproportion'd thought his act.
Be **thou** familiar, but by no means vulgar;
Those friends **thou** hast, and their adoption tried,
Grapple them unto **thy** soul with hoops of steel.
Give every man **thy** ear, but few **thy** voice;
Neither a borrower nor a lender be,
For loan oft loses both itself and friend.
This above all, to **thine** own self be true,
And it must follow as the night the day
Thou canst not then be false to any man.
Farewell, my blessing season this in **thee**.

LAERTES

Most humbly do I take my leave, my lord.

POLONIUS

The time invests **you**; go, **your** servants tend.

LAERTES

    Farewell, Ophelia, and remember well

    What I have said to **you**.

OPHELIA   'Tis in my memory lock'd,

    And **you** alone shall keep the key of it.

LAERTES

    Farewell.

Exit

POLONIUS

    What is't, Ophelia, he hath said to **you**?

OPHELIA

    So please **you**, something touching the Lord Hamlet.

POLONIUS

    Marry, well bethought.

    'Tis told me he hath very oft of late

    Given private time to **you**, and **you yourself**

    Have of **your** audience been most free and bounteous.

    If it be so – and so 'tis put on me,

    And that in way of caution – I must tell **you**

    You do not understand **yourself** so clearly

    As it behoves my daughter and **your** honour.

    What is between **you**? Give me up the truth.

OPHELIA

    He hath, my lord, of late made many tenders

    Of his affection to me.

POLONIUS

    Affection? Pooh, **you** speak like a green girl,

Unsifted in such perilous circumstance.
Do **you** believe his tenders, as **you** call them?

OPHELIA

I do not know, my lord, what I should think.

POLONIUS

Marry, I will teach **you**, think **yourself** a baby
That **you** have ta'en these tenders for true pay
Which are not sterling. Tender **yourself** more dearly.
Or **you**'ll tender me a fool

OPHELIA

My lord, he hath importuned me with love
In honourable fashion

POLONIUS

Ay, fashion **you** may call it. Go to, go to

OPHELIA

And hath given countenance to his speech, my lord,
With almost all the holy vows of heaven.

POLONIUS

Ay, springes to catch woodcocks. I do know
When the blood burns, how prodigal the soul
Lends the tongue vows.
[...]
                    This is for all,
I would not, in plain terms, from this time forth
Have **you** so slander any moment leisure
As to give words or talk with the Lord Hamlet.
Look to't I charge **you**. Come **your** ways.

OPHELIA

I shall obey, my lord.

Exeunt

Act this scene out and discuss the following:

- What reasons might there be for Polonius to use **thou** to his son and **you** to his daughter?

- How might that difference affect the staging and mood of the two pieces of dialogue?

- At one point (the third line of this extract) Polonius uses **you** to Laertes at the start of the line and **thee** at the end of it. What motivates that change?

- Consult the **Commentary** (p. 117) and try the scene again.

Session six: Married love

Texts: *Macbeth* Act 1 Scene 7 (Macbeth and Lady Macbeth)
Henry IV Part One Act 2 Scene 3 (Hotspur and Lady Percy)

Married couples do not use **thou** to each other routinely but some couples use it more than others and, as in other relationships, they may use it for moments of particular affection, or in angry argument. The pronouns that married couples use to each other tell us a good deal about their relationships.

Exercise 1: Why the switch?

Try walking through the scene below between Macbeth and Lady Macbeth.

Macbeth Act 1 Scene 7, 28–62.
(Influenced by the prophecy of witches that Macbeth will become king, he and his wife plan to murder King Duncan, who is a guest in their castle. However, Macbeth is having pangs of conscience.)

Enter LADY MACBETH

MACBETH
How now! What news?

LADY MACBETH
He hath almost supp'd. Why have **you** left the chamber?

MACBETH
Hath he ask'd for me?

LADY MACBETH   Know **you** not he hath?

MACBETH

> We will proceed no further in this business.
> He hath honoured me of late; and I have bought
> Golden opinions from all sorts of people,
> Which would be worn now in their newest gloss,
> Not cast aside so soon.

LADY MACBETH   Was the hope drunk

> Wherein **you** dress'd **yourself**? Hath it slept since?
> And wakes it now to look so green and pale
> At what it did so freely? From this time
> Such I account **thy** love. Art **thou** afeard
> To be the same in **thine** own act and valour
> As **thou** art in desire? Would'st **thou** have that
> Which **thou** esteem'st the ornament of life,
> And live a coward in **thine** own esteem,
> Letting 'I dare not' wait upon 'I would',
> Like the poor cat i'th' adage?

MACBETH   **Prithee**, peace!

> I dare do all that may become a man;
> Who dares do more is none.

LADY MACBETH   What beast was't then

> That made **you** break this enterprise to me?
> When **you** durst do it then **you** were a man:
> And to be more than what **you** were, **you** would
> Be so much more the man. Nor time nor place
> Did then adhere, and yet **you** would make both:
> They have made themselves, and that their fitness now
> Hath unmade **you**. I have given suck, and know
> How tender 'tis to love the babe that milks me:

I would, while it was smiling in my face,
Have pluck'd my nipple from his boneless gums,
And dash'd the brains out, had I so sworn
As **you** have done to this.

MACBETH   If we should fail?

LADY MACBETH   We fail!
But screw **your** courage to the sticking place
And we'll not fail. When Duncan is asleep
(Whereto the rather his day's hard journey
Shall soundly invite him) his two chamberlains
Will I with wine and wassail so convince
That memory, the warder of the brain,
Shall be a fume. When in swinish sleep
Their drenched natures lie, as in a death,
What cannot **you** and I perform
Upon the unguarded Duncan? What not put upon
His spongy officers, who shall bear the guilt
Of our great quell?

MACBETH   Bring forth men children only!
For **thy** undaunted mettle should compose
Nothing but males!
I am settled and bend up
Each corporal agent to this terrible feat.
Away, and mock the time with fairest show:
False face must hide what the false heart doth know.

Discussion

- Lady Macbeth switches to **thou** in just one speech and then switches back to **you**. What do you think motivates these changes?

- Do these switches suggest anything about the staging of the scene?

- What might be the reasons for Macbeth's one **thy** to Lady Macbeth at the end of the scene?

- Lady Macbeth never uses **thou** to Macbeth after this scene. If you know the play, suggest why this might be.

Now turn to the **Commentary** (p. 122), discuss how you might want to stage the scene and act it out again.

Exercise 2: Loves me/loves me not

(You will need highlighter pens or coloured pencils for this exercise)
Read through the scene between Harry Percy (Hotspur) and his wife.

Henry IV Part One Act 2 Scene 3, 73–117.
(Hotspur is making secret preparations to raise a rebellion against the King. His wife, Lady Percy, knows that something is preoccupying him, suspects what his plans are and is determined to find out the truth from him.)

LADY PERCY

    Tell me, sweet lord, what is't that takes from **thee**
    Thy stomach, pleasure and **thy** golden sleep?
    Some heavy business hath my lord in hand,
    And I must know it, else he loves me not.

HOTSPUR

    What ho!

Enter a SERVANT
Is Gilliams with the packet gone?

SERVANT

    He is, my lord, an hour ago.

HOTSPUR

Bid Butler lead my horse into the park.

Exit SERVANT

LADY PERCY

But hear **you**, my lord.

HOTSPUR

What say'st **thou**, my lady?

LADY PERCY

What is it carries **you** away?

HOTSPUR

Why, my horse, my love, my horse.

LADY PERCY

Out, **you** mad-headed ape!

A weasel hath not such a deal of spleen

As **you** are toss'd with. In faith,

I'll know **your** business, Harry, that I will;

I fear my brother Mortimer doth stir

About his title, and hath sent for **you**

To line his enterprise. But if **you** go –

HOTSPUR

So far afoot I shall be weary, love.

LADY PERCY

Come, come, **you** paraquito, answer me

Directly unto this question that I ask.

In faith, I'll break **thy** little finger, Harry.

And if **thou** wilt not tell me all things true.

HOTSPUR

> Away, away, **you** trifler! Love! I love **thee** not,
> I care not for **thee**, Kate; this is no world
> To play with mammets, and to tilt with lips;
> We must have bloody noses and crack'd crowns.
> What say'st **thou**, Kate? What would'st **thou** have with me?

LADY PERCY

> Do **you** not love me? Do **you** not indeed?
> Well, do not then, for since **you** love me not
> I will not love myself. Do **you** not love me?
> Nay, tell me if **you** speak in jest or no.

HOTSPUR

> Come, wilt **thou** see me ride?
> And when I am a horseback I will swear
> I love **thee** infinitely. But hark **you** Kate,
> I must not have **you** henceforth question me
> Whither I go, nor reason whereabout:
> Whither I must I must; and, to conclude,
> This evening must I leave **you** gentle Kate.
> I know **you** wise, but yet no farther wise
> Than Harry Percy's wife; constant **you** are,
> But yet a woman, and for secrecy
> No lady closer, for I well believe
> **Thou** wilt not utter what **thou** dost not know;
> And so far will I trust **thee**, gentle Kate.

LADY PERCY

> How? So far?

HOTSPUR

>Not an inch further. But hear **you**, Kate,
>Whither I go, thither shall **you** go too:
>Today will I set forth, tomorrow **you**.
>Will that content **you**, Kate?

LADY PERCY   It must, of force.

Exeunt

- Using highlighter pens or underlining, highlight the **you** forms and the **thou** forms in different colours. Then look at the names the couple use to each other, using the colour with which you have marked the **you** forms to highlight respectful use of formal names, and the colour used for **thou** forms to highlight endearments or insulting names.

- Consider the patterns that you find. How do you explain the switches between **you** and **thou**?

- We expect to see formal or respectful names to go with **you**, and affectionate, intimate or insulting names to go with **thou**. How many mismatches can you find between name and pronoun in this extract?

- What do the mismatches suggest about the couple's feelings for one another?

- How will these mismatches help actors to play the scene?

Now walk through the scene.

Consult the **Commentary** (p. 125) and walk the scene through again if you feel that will be helpful.

Session seven: Freudian slips and testing moments

Texts: *Love's Labour's Lost* Act 2 Scene 1 (The King of Navarre to the
Princess of France)
As You Like It Act 5 Scene 2 (Rosalind to Orlando)
Romeo and Juliet Act 3 Scene 5 (Romeo to Juliet)
Hamlet Act 3 Scene 1 (Hamlet to Ophelia)
Othello Act 3 Scene 4 (Othello to Desdemona)
A Midsummer Night's Dream Act 2 Scene 1 (Oberon to Titania)

Exercise 1: Freudian slips: What's the secret?

Since **thou** is the emotional pronoun, characters reveal themselves
particularly through its use. Generally they are in control of how they
use it, expressing their love, their anger and so on, but occasionally
they slip into it inadvertently, revealing more, perhaps, than they
intended to.

Love's Labour's Lost Act 2 Scene 1, 168–78.
*(The young King of Navarre has taken a pledge, with his three closest
friends, to turn the royal court into a place of serious study – 'a little
academe' – where they will live a monastic life, and where women will
be banned from entering. However, the Princess of France has been sent
by her elderly father on an embassy to demand that Navarre returns the
province of Aquitaine, and the King has been obliged to see her. Because
of his vow, however, they have met in the grounds outside his palace. In
this extract, the discussion is coming to an end.)*

KING

    Meantime, receive such welcome at my hand
    As honour, without breach of honour, may

Make tender of to **thy** true worthiness.

You may not come, fair Princess, within my gates,

But here without **you** shall be so received

As **you** shall deem **yourself** lodged in my heart,

Though so denied fair harbour in my house.

Your own good thoughts excuse me, and farewell.

Tomorrow we shall visit **you** again.

PRINCESS

Sweet health and fair desires consort **your** grace.

KING

Thy own wish wish I **thee** in every place.

Discussion

- What do the King's switches to **thou** forms suggest about the way the whole scene might be played?

- What do the **thy** and **thee** in his final speech suggest about the staging of the King's exit?

- Walk through the scene, trying out your ideas before consulting the **Commentary** (p. 105).

As You Like It, Act 5 Scene 2, 19–27.

(Rosalind – in love with Orlando, but still pretending to be the boy, Ganymede – fainted when she heard that Orlando had been wounded by a lion in the forest and was shown the bloodstained handkerchief that had been wrapped round the wound. Now she sees Orlando with his arm in a sling.)

ROSALIND

O my dear Orlando, how it grieves me to see **thee** wear **thy** heart in a scarf!

ORLANDO

It is my arm.

ROSALIND

I thought **thy** heart had been wounded with the claws of a lion.

ORLANDO

Wounded it is but with the eyes of a lady.

ROSALIND

Did **your** brother tell **you** how I counterfeited to swoon when he showed me **your** handkerchief?

ORLANDO

Ay, and greater wonders than that.

Discussion

• Rosalind unguardedly shows her true feelings for Orlando when she sees him wounded. She returns to her usual **you** but why do you think she starts talking about the fact that she fainted earlier?

Perform the extract, then look at the **Commentary** (p. 131) and perform the extract again if you would like to change anything.

Romeo and Juliet Act 3 Scene 5, 48–59.
(Romeo has been banished from Verona. After one secret night with Juliet he is leaving her, climbing down from her bedroom balcony. This is the last exchange between them.)

ROMEO

Farewell.

I will omit no opportunity

That may convey my greetings, love, to **thee**

JULIET

O think'st **thou** we shall ever meet again?

ROMEO

I doubt it not, and all these woes shall serve

For sweet discourses in our time to come.

JULIET

O God, I have an ill-divining soul.

Methinks I see **thee** now **thou** art below

As one dead in the bottom of a tomb.

Either my eyesight fails or **thou** look'st pale.

ROMEO

And trust me, love, in my eyes so do **you**.

Dry sorrow drinks our blood. Adieu, adieu.

Exit

- Discuss what reasons there might be for Romeo's last word to Juliet to be '**you**', when he has always used **thou** to her up to this point.

- Perform the extract, then consult the **Commentary** (p. 130) and consider whether this makes any difference to the way Romeo might speak his last lines.

Exercise 2: Testing moments: What's the twist?

In each of the following exchanges, the man makes a switch to a different pronoun at a crucial moment – a switch which seems to be designed to wrong-foot the woman. In the texts below, the 'rogue' pronoun has been changed to the pronoun that the man uses elsewhere.

- Read through each exchange and decide where you think the switch of pronoun occurs, Then consult the **Commentary** (p. 133) and act out each exchange.

Hamlet Act 3 Scene 1, 121–38.
(Anxious to find out the cause of Hamlet's 'madness', Polonius and the King have hidden themselves to eavesdrop on a conversation between Hamlet and Ophelia. Ophelia knows that they are there.)

HAMLET

Get **thee** to a nunnery. Why wouldst **thou** be a breeder of sinners? I am myself indifferent honest, but yet I could accuse me of such things that it were better my mother had not borne me. I am very proud, revengeful, ambitious, with more offences at my beck than I have thoughts to put them in, imagination to give them shape, or time to act them in. What should such fellows as I do crawling between earth and heaven? We are arrant knaves all, believe none of us. Go **thy** ways to a nunnery. Where's **thy** father?

OPHELIA

At home, my lord.

HAMLET

Let the doors be shut upon him, that he may play the fool nowhere but in's own house. Farewell.

OPHELIA

O help him, **you** sweet heavens.

HAMLET

If **thou** dost marry, I'll give **thee** this plague for **thy** dowry, be **thou** as chaste as ice, as pure as snow, **thou** shalt not escape calumny. Get **thee** to a nunnery. Farewell.

Othello Act 3 Scene 4, 32–57 (abridged text).

(Othello has been sent as general to command the Venetian forces in Cyprus and has taken his new wife, Desdemona, with him. Iago, who hates Othello and is determined to destroy him, has set out to convince Othello that his wife is having an affair with Cassio, a disgraced officer in the army. Iago has stolen a handkerchief that Othello gave to Desdemona and has told Othello that Desdemona has given the handkerchief to Cassio.)

OTHELLO

How do **you**, Desdemona?

DESDEMONA   Well, my good lord.

OTHELLO

Give me **your** hand. This hand is moist, my lady.

DESDEMONA

It hath felt no age, nor known no sorrow.

OTHELLO

[...]

'Tis a good hand,

A frank one.

DESDEMONA   **You** may indeed say so,

For 'twas that hand that gave away my heart.

Come now, **your** promise.

OTHELLO

What promise, chuck?

DESDEMONA

I have sent to bid Cassio come speak with **you**.

OTHELLO

I have a salt and sullen rheum offends me.

Lend me **your** handkerchief.

DESDEMONA   Here, my lord.

OTHELLO

That which I gave **you**.

DESDEMONA   I have it not about me.

OTHELLO

Not?

DESDEMONA   No, faith, my lord.

OTHELLO

That's a fault.

A Midsummer Night's Dream Act 2 Scene 1, 118–45 (abridged text). *(Oberon and Titania, the King and Queen of the Fairies, are in conflict over the custody of a little changeling boy. Titania has been lamenting the fact that their discord has had a disastrous effect on human lives, causing upsets in the weather and destruction of crops.)*

OBERON

Do **you** amend it then: it lies in **you**.

Why should Titania cross her Oberon?

I do but beg a little changeling boy

To be my henchman.

TITANIA   Set **your** heart at rest.

The fairy land buys not the child of me

His mother was a votaress of my order

[...]

But she, being mortal, of that child did die,
And for her sake do I rear up her boy,
And for her sake I will not part with him.

OBERON

How long within this wood intend **you** stay?

TITANIA

Perchance till after Theseus' wedding day.
If **you** will patiently dance in our round,
And see our moonlight revels, go with us;
If not, shun me, and I will spare **your** haunts.

OBERON

Give me that boy, and I will go with **you**.

TITANIA

Not for **your** fairy kingdom. Fairies, away.
We shall chide downright if I longer stay.

Exeunt TITANIA *and her train*

Session eight: Absent friends

Texts: *Julius Caesar* Act 3 Scene 1 (Mark Antony)
Julius Caesar Act 3 Scene 1 (Mark Antony)
King Lear Act 4 Scene 7 (Cordelia)
Macbeth Act 3 Scene 1 (Banquo)
Much Ado About Nothing Act 3 Scene 1 (Beatrice)

All the uses of **thou** that we have looked at so far reflect its use in the everyday language of the time: they are not a literary or dramatic convention but share the speech patterns that can be found in letters, dictated wills, trial transcripts and so on. In this last session, however, we are dealing with a dramatic convention. We are dealing with a rhetorical use of **thou** – the use for forms of address that are quite rare in everyday speech but are a recognized dramatic trope: address to abstract entities (love, fortune, death, the moon), to non-human entities (gods, animals), and to human beings who are not able to hear what is being said (the sleeping, the dead, and those who are not actually on stage at the time). It is this last group – these 'absent' humans – which is, perhaps, the most interesting one because, in deploying the convention of **thou** address, characters also invoke the other meanings of **thou**. For various reasons they would not be able to use **thou** if their addressee were present and conscious, but the rhetorical convention gives them the freedom to express aloud powerful emotions for which **thou** is fitting.

Exercise 1: How do I feel?

There are four examples to consider here: one to a sleeping figure, one to a dead one, and two to absent addressees.

- In each case, read through the speech and consider why the speaker would not normally use **thou** to this addressee.

- What does the freedom to use **thou** in each case express about their hidden feelings?

Julius Caesar Act 3 Scene 1, 185–203.
(Caesar has just been assassinated in the Senate. His killers are standing round his dead body and Mark Antony, Caesar's favourite, who was not one of the killers, has been persuaded to make his peace with them and join them in the new government. He shakes their bloody hands.)

ANTONY

First, Marcus Brutus, will I shake with **you**.
Next, Caius Cassius, do I take **your** hand.
Now, Decius Brutus, **yours**. Now **yours**, Metellus.
Yours, Cinna, and my valiant Casca, **yours**.
Though last, not least in love, **yours** good Trebonius.
Gentlemen all, alas, what shall I say?
My credit now stands on such slippery ground
That one of two bad ways **you** must conceit me,
Either a coward or a flatterer.
That I did love **thee**, Caesar, O 'tis true:
If then **thy** spirit look upon us now,
Shall it not grieve **thee** dearer than **thy** death
To see **thy** Antony making his peace,
Shaking the bloody fingers of **thy** foes,
Most noble in the presence of **thy** corpse.
Had I as many eyes as **thou** hast wounds
Weeping as fast as they stream forth **thy** blood,
It would become me better than to close
In terms of friendship with **thine** enemies.

Julius Caesar Act 3 Scene 1, 254–75 (abridged text).
(After discussing the arrangements for Caesar's funeral, the assassins depart, leaving Antony alone with Caesar's body.)

ANTONY

O pardon me, **thou** bleeding piece of earth,
That I am meek and gentle with these butchers.
Thou art the ruins of the noblest man
That ever lived in the tide of times.
Woe to the hand that shed this costly blood.
Over **thy** wounds now I do prophesy,
A curse shall light upon the limbs of men:
Domestic fury and fierce civil strife
Shall cumber all the parts of Italy;
[...]
And Caesar's spirit, ranging for revenge,
With Ate by his side, come hot from hell,
Shall in these confines, with a monarch's voice,
Cry havoc, and let slip the dogs of war.

King Lear Act 4 Scene 7, 26–44 (abridged text).
*(King Lear, having given up his power to his two elder daughters, has
been barred from both their houses and left destitute and insane. He has
been rescued by Kent and is now being treated by doctors who have
given him a sleeping draught. Cordelia, banished earlier by her father,
has returned to help him. She finds him sleeping.)*

CORDELIA

O my dear father, restoration hang
Thy medicine on my lips, and let this kiss
Repair those violent harms that my two sisters
Have in **thy** reverence made.

[...]

        and wast **thou** fain, poor father,
To hovel **thee** with swine and rogues forlorn

In short and musty straw? Alack, alack!

'Tis wonder that **thy** life and wits at once

Had not concluded all. He wakes.

How does my royal lord? How fares **your** majesty?

Macbeth Act 3 Scene 1, 1–18.

(Banquo was with Macbeth when they met the three witches who promised Macbeth that he would be king. They promised Banquo that his children would be kings. At this point in the play, King Duncan has been found murdered and Macbeth has just been proclaimed king. Banquo is alone on stage.)

BANQUO

 Thou hast it now, King, Cawdor, Glamis, all,

 As the weird women promis'd; and, I fear,

 Thou play'dst most foully for't; yet it was said

 It should not stand in **thy** posterity;

 But that myself should be the root and father

 Of many kings. If there come truth from them

 (As upon **thee**, Macbeth, their speeches shine),

 Why, on the verities on **thee** made good,

 May they not be my oracles as well,

 And set me up in hope? But hush, no more.

 Sennet sounded. Enter MACBETH *as King,* LADY MACBETH
   as Queen, LENNOX, ROSS, *lords and attendants.*

MACBETH

 Here's our chief guest.

LADY MACBETH   If he had been forgotten

 It had been as a gap in our great feast

 And all things unbecoming.

MACBETH

> Tonight we hold a solemn supper, Sir,
> And I'll request **your** presence.

BANQUO   Let **your** highness

> Command upon me, to the which my duties
> Are with a most indissoluble tie
> Forever knit.

Much Ado About Nothing Act 3 Scene 1, 107–16.
(The friends of Beatrice and Benedick have plotted to bring them together. Beatrice's friends have just arranged for her to 'overhear' a conversation in which they have discussed how much Benedick is in love with her. Following their exit, Beatrice is left alone on stage.)

BEATRICE

> What fire is in mine ears? Can this be true?
> Stand I condemned for pride and scorn so much?
> Contempt, farewell, and maiden pride adieu!
> No glory lives behind the back of such.
> And, Benedick, love on, I will requite **thee**,
> Taming my wild heart to **thy** loving hand.
> If **thou** dost love, my kindness shall incite **thee**
> To bind our loves up in a holy band;
> For others say **thou** dost deserve, and I
> Believe it better than reportingly.

Exit

Now consult the **Commentary** p. 138.

3
Commentary

Session one: Best friends

Exercise 1: *As You Like It* Act 1 Scene 2, 1–23 (abridged text).

CELIA

> I pray *thee* Rosalind, sweet my coz, be merry.

ROSALIND

> Dear Celia, I show more mirth than I am mistress of, and would
> **you** yet I were merrier?
> [...]

CELIA

> Herein I see *thou* lov'st me not with the full weight that I love
> *thee*. If my uncle, *thy* banished father, had banished *thy* uncle,
> the Duke my father, so *thou* hadst been with me, I could have
> taught my love to take *thy* father for mine. So wouldst *thou* if
> the truth of *thy* love to me were as righteously tempered as mine
> is to *thee*

ROSALIND

> Well, I will forget the condition of my estate to rejoice in **yours**.

CELIA

> **You** know my father hath no child but I, nor none is like to have; and truly, when he dies, *thou* shalt be his heir, for what he hath taken away from *thy* father perforce I will render *thee* again in affection. By mine honour I will, and when I break that oath, let me turn monster. Therefore my sweet Rose, my dear Rose, be merry.

ROSALIND

> From henceforth I will, coz, and devise sports. Let me see, what think **you** of falling in love?

Rosalind and Celia are close and affectionate cousins – we learn that Celia's father would have sent Rosalind into exile with her father when he usurped the dukedom if Celia had not begged him to let her stay. Now, though, she finds herself in a difficult situation: she has displaced Rosalind as the heir to the dukedom, and Rosalind is living at court on sufferance and is unhappy. Celia is desperate to reassure her that she loves her as much as ever, so it is not surprising that she uses the intimate **thou** pronouns to her, but she uses them perhaps too much. The stepping exercise sees her backing Rosalind physically into a corner – a demonstration of the emotional 'crowding' that she is doing. She is over eager and that can feel like too much pressure.

Why doesn't Rosalind respond with **thou** in return? Perhaps it is a reaction to Celia's emotional pressure – she doesn't want to be forced into shrugging off her unhappiness; perhaps she does feel some resentment towards Celia – withholding from using **thou** gives her a kind of power, and the more formal **you** could even be ironic, a respectful address to the new heir to the dukedom; perhaps she is just sad and hasn't the spirit for **thou**. **Thou** is an energetic pronoun – it goes with high emotion and self-confidence. An actor playing Rosalind can explore all these possibilities in deciding how she might play the scene.

Exercise 2: *As You Like It* Act 3 Scene 2, 176–223.

CELIA

Trow **you** who hath done this?

ROSALIND

Is it a man?

CELIA

And a chain that **you** once wore about his neck. Change **you** colour?

ROSALIND

I *prithee* who?

CELIA

O Lord, Lord, it is a hard matter for friends to meet, but mountains may be removed with earthquakes, and so encounter.

ROSALIND

Nay but who is it?

CELIA

Is it possible?

ROSALIND

Nay, I *prithee* now with the most petitionary vehemence, tell me who it is.

CELIA

O wonderful, wonderful, and most wonderful, wonderful, and yet again wonderful, and after that out of all whooping!

ROSALIND

Good my complexion! Dost *thou* think because I am caparisoned like a man I have a doublet and hose in my disposition? One inch of delay more is a South Sea of discovery. I *prithee* tell me who is it quickly, and speak apace. I would *thou* couldst stammer, that *thou* might'st pour the concealed man out of *thy* mouth, as wine comes out of a narrow-mouthed bottle, either too much at once or none at all. I *prithee* take the cork out of *thy* mouth that I may drink *thy* tidings.

CELIA

So **you** may put a man in **your** belly.

ROSALIND

Is he of God's making? What manner of man? Is his head worth a hat? Or his chin worth a beard?

CELIA

Nay he hath but a little beard.

ROSALIND

Why, God will send more if the man will be thankful. Let me stay the growth of his beard if *thou* delay me not the knowledge of his chin.

CELIA

It is young Orlando, that tripped up the wrestler's heels and **your** heart both in an instant.

ROSALIND

Nay, but the devil take mocking! Speak sad brow and true maid.

CELIA

I'faith, coz, 'tis he.

ROSALIND

Orlando?

CELIA

Orlando.

ROSALIND

Alas the day! What shall I do with my doublet and hose? What did he when *thou* saw'st him? What said he? How looked he? Wherein went he? What makes he here? Did he ask for me? Where remains he? How parted he with *thee* and when shalt *thou* see him again? Answer me in one word.

CELIA

You must borrow me Gargantua's mouth first. 'Tis a word too great for any mouth of this age's size!

In this extract the pronouns are reversed. Now all the emotional energy comes from Rosalind. She is now begging Celia for understanding, lit up with the excitement of learning that Orlando is in the forest and that he loves her. High emotions of all kinds – love, anger, fear, contempt, despair – are likely to be expressed with **thou**.

Why does Celia not respond with **thou** in return? She now has the power – she knows more than Rosalind – and she is playing a game with her. By using **you** she pretends to be detached, not to be engaged with Rosalind's excitement. The contrasting pronouns can give an extra edge to the comedy of the scene.

Exercise 3: *The Merchant of Venice* Act 2 Scene 2, 166–95.

GRATIANO

Signior Bassanio!

BASSANIO   Gratiano!

GRATIANO

I have a suit to **you**.

BASSANIO   **You** have obtain'd it.

GRATIANO

    You must not deny me, I must go with **you** to Belmont.

BASSANIO

    Why then **you** must – but hear **thee** Gratiano,
    Thou art too wild, too rude and bold of voice,
    Parts that become **thee** happily enough,
    And in such eyes as ours appear not faults –
    But where **thou** art not known – why there they show
    Something too liberal – pray **thee** take pain
    To allay with some cold drops of modesty
    Thy skipping spirit, lest through **thy** wild behaviour
    I be misconst'red in the place I go to,
    And lose my hopes.

GRATIANO   Signior Bassanio, hear me –
    If I do not put on a sober habit,
    Talk with respect, and swear but now and then,
    Wear prayer books in my pocket, look demurely,
    Nay more, while grace is saying hood mine eyes
    Thus with my hat, and sigh and say 'Amen':
    Use all the observance of civility
    Like one well studied in a sad ostent
    To please his grandam, never trust me more.

BASSANIO

    Well, we shall see **your** bearing.

GRATIANO

    Nay but I bar tonight, **you** shall not gauge me
    By what we do tonight.

BASSANIO No that were pity,
I would entreat **you** rather to put on
Your boldest suit of mirth, for we have friends
That purpose merriment; but fare **you** well,
I have some business.

There are at least two ways that an actor might choose to play Bassanio's switch to using **thou** when he is warning Gratiano to moderate his behaviour if he goes with him to Belmont. It seems that **you** is their usual pronoun to each other, since Bassanio goes back to using it once his homily is over, so there is something special about the **thou** use for this one speech.

We can notice that Gratiano addresses Bassanio as 'Signor Bassanio', a respectful form of address, which may be because he wants a favour from him but may also suggest that they are not close friends and that Bassanio may have higher social status (later in the play, Bassanio wins the Lady Portia and Gratiano is happy to marry Nerissa, her waiting gentlewoman). So, in using **thou** to give him his instructions Bassanio could be pulling rank socially, and he could be playing on the power dynamic between them – he has the power to grant or refuse Gratiano's request.

On the other hand, Bassanio's language in the speech is not harsh: he admits that Gratiano's manners 'in such eyes as ours appear not faults' and he asks, 'pray **thee** take pain' rather than issuing an order. So, we can see Bassanio's **thou**s as softening what he says to Gratiano: he needs to tell him that his usual behaviour will not do in Belmont but still to assure him of his friendship by using the intimate pronoun to acknowledge their friendship.

The multiple uses of **thou** make both interpretations possible. Try acting out the scene both ways.

Session two: Too wise to woo peaceably

Exercise 1: *Much Ado About Nothing* Act 4 Scene 1, 250–334 (abridged text).

BENEDICK

Lady Beatrice, have **you** wept all this while?

BEATRICE

Yea, and I will weep a while longer.

BENEDICK

I will not desire that.

BEATRICE

You have no reason, I do it freely

BENEDICK

Surely I do believe **your** fair cousin is wronged

BEATRICE

Ah, how much might the man deserve of me that would right her!

BENEDICK

Is there any way to show such friendship?

BEATRICE

A very even way, but no such friend.

BENEDICK

May a man do it?

BEATRICE

It is a man's office, but not **yours**.

BENEDICK

I do love nothing in the world so well as **you** – is not that strange?

BEATRICE

As strange as the thing I know not. It were as possible for me to say I loved nothing so well as **you**, but believe me not, I confess nothing, nor I deny nothing. I am sorry for my cousin.

BENEDICK

By my sword, Beatrice, **thou** lovest me

BEATRICE

Do not swear and eat it

BENEDICK

I will swear by it that **you** love me, and will make him eat it that swears I love not **you**.

BEATRICE

Will **you** not eat **your** word?

BENEDICK

With no sauce that can be devised to it. I protest I love **thee**.

BEATRICE

Why then, God forgive me!

BENEDICK

What offence, sweet Beatrice?

BEATRICE

You have stayed me in a happy hour, I was about to protest I loved **you**.

BENEDICK

And do it with all **thy** heart.

BEATRICE

I love **you** with so much of my heart that none is left to protest.

BENEDICK

Come, bid me do anything for **thee**.

BEATRICE

Kill Claudio!

BENEDICK

Ha, not for the wide world!

BEATRICE

You kill me to deny it. Farewell.

BENEDICK

Tarry, sweet Beatrice.

BEATRICE

I am gone, though I am here; there is no love in **you**; nay I pray **you** let me go.

BENEDICK

Beatrice –

BEATRICE

In faith, I will go.

BENEDICK

We'll be friends first.

BEATRICE

You dare easier be friends with me than fight with mine enemy.

BENEDICK

Is Claudio **thine** enemy?

BEATRICE

Is he not approved in the height a villain, that hath slandered, scorned, dishonoured my kinswoman? O that I were a man! What, bear her in hand until they come to take hands, and then with public accusation, uncovered slander, unmitigated rancour – O God that I were a man! I would eat his heart in the market-place.

BENEDICK

Hear me, Beatrice.

BEATRICE

Talk with a man out at a window! A proper saying!

BENEDICK

Nay, but Beatrice –

BEATRICE

Sweet Hero! She is wronged, she is slandered, she is undone.

[...]

BENEDICK

Tarry, good Beatrice. By this hand I love **thee**.

BEATRICE

Use it for my love some other way than swearing by it.

BENEDICK

Think **you** in **your** soul the Count Claudio hath wronged Hero?

BEATRICE

Yea, as sure as I have a thought, or a soul.

BENEDICK

> Enough! I am engaged, I will challenge him. I will kiss **your** hand, and so I leave **you**. By this hand Claudio shall render me a dear account. Go comfort **your** cousin; I must say she is dead; and so farewell.

Before this scene, there has been a great deal of verbal sparring between Beatrice and Benedick, in which they have been quite insulting to one another but have never used **thou** in a contemptuous way. Now, each of them has admitted (to themselves and to the audience) that they love the other. Believing that Beatrice loves him, Benedick wants to declare his love for her, though he has chosen a bad time. Beatrice's distress and preoccupation about Hero's disgrace might be an explanation for her not using **thou** and not expressing wholehearted love back. We can see how Benedick starts with **you**, and calls her 'Lady Beatrice' – respectful titles go with **you**, while insulting names or endearments go with **thou**. Benedick takes a while to pluck up the courage to use **thou** and then stays with it even when Beatrice changes the subject to Hero's situation. However, at the end, when Benedick declares seriously that he will challenge Claudio, he switches to **you**. He signals that he is no longer playing the courtship game but is in deadly earnest.

Exercise 2: *Much Ado About Nothing* Act 5 Scene 2, 42–97 (abridged text).

Enter BEATRICE

BENEDICK

> Sweet Beatrice, wouldst **thou** come when I called **thee**?

BEATRICE

> Yea, signor, and depart when **you** bid me.

BENEDICK

O, stay but till then.

BEATRICE

'Then' is spoken: fare **you** well now. And yet ere I go, let me go with that I came, which is, with knowing what hath passed between **you** and Claudio.

BENEDICK

Only foul words – and thereupon I will kiss **thee**.

BEATRICE

Foul words is but foul wind, and foul wind is but foul breath and foul breath is noisome, therefore I will depart unkissed.

BENEDICK

Thou has frighted the word out of his right sense, so forcible is **thy** wit. But I must tell **thee** plainly, Claudio undergoes my challenge, and either I must shortly hear from him, or I will subscribe him a coward. And I pray **thee** now tell me, for which of my bad parts didst **thou** first fall in love with me?

BEATRICE

For them all together, which maintained so politic a state of evil that they will not admit any good part to intermingle with them. But for which of my good parts did **you** first suffer love for me?

BENEDICK

'Suffer love' – a good epithet! I do suffer love indeed, for I love **thee** against my will.

BEATRICE

In spite of **your** heart, I think. Alas, poor heart! If **you** will spite it for my sake, I will spite it for **yours**, for I will never love that which my friend hates.

BENEDICK

Thou and I are too wise to woo peaceably.

BEATRICE

It appears not in this confession: there's not one wise man among twenty that will praise himself.

[...]

BENEDICK

So much for praising myself, who I myself will bear witness is praiseworthy. And now tell me, how doth **your** cousin?

BEATRICE

Very ill.

BENEDICK

And how do **you**?

BEATRICE

Very ill too.

BENEDICK

Serve God, love me, and mend. There will I leave **you** too, for here comes one in haste.

Enter URSULA

URSULA

Madam, **you** must come to **your** uncle – yonder's old coil at home. It is proved my Lady Hero hath been falsely accused, the Prince and Claudio mightily abused, and Don John is the author of all, who is fled and gone. Will **you** come presently?

BEATRICE

Will **you** go hear this news signior?

BENEDICK

I will live in **thy** heart, die in **thy** lap and be buried in **thy** eyes: and moreover, I will go with **thee** to **thy** uncle's.

Exeunt

The situation has moved on by the time Beatrice and Benedick meet here. Benedick, having challenged Claudio as Beatrice asked, feels that he is now her acknowledged suitor, so he starts immediately with **thou** (notice, she is now 'sweet' Beatrice, rather than 'Lady' Beatrice). He goes on using **thou**, and only changes to **you** when he asks about Hero. This is similar to his change in 4.1, when he says he will challenge Claudio. For Benedick, **thou** is used when he is playing a love scene, or doing the courtship dance, but he switches to **you** for serious issues. Why does Beatrice still not use **thou**? She is quite happy to indulge in lovers' talk here, but doesn't meet **thou** with **thou**. An actor playing her will want to think about this. Perhaps her rejection by Benedick in the past has cut deep and she has developed a protective shell, so she keeps to the more reserved **you** to hide the depth of her feelings. (In fact, she never uses **thou** to Benedick, except in her soliloquy, when he is not there: 'Then Benedick love on, I will requite **thee**'.)

Exercise 3: *The Taming of the Shrew* Act 2 Scene 1, 183–274.

Enter KATHERINA

PETRUCHIO

Good morrow Kate, for that's **your** name, I hear.

KATHERINA

Well have **you** heard, but something hard of hearing;
They call me Katherine that do talk of me.

PETRUCHIO

> **You** lie, in faith, for **you** are call'd plain Kate,
> And bonny Kate and sometimes Kate the curst;
> But Kate, the prettiest Kate in Christendom,
> Kate of Kate Hall, my super-dainty Kate,
> For dainties are all Kates, and therefore, Kate,
> Take this of me, Kate of my consolation,
> Hearing **thy** mildness prais'd in every town,
> **Thy** virtues spoke of, and **thy** beauty sounded,
> Yet not so deeply as to **thee** belongs,
> Myself am mov'd to woo **thee** for my wife.

KATHERINA

> Mov'd in good time! Let him that mov'd **you** hither
> Remove **you** hence. I knew **you** at the first
> **You** were a movable.

PETRUCHIO   Why, what's a movable?

KATHERINA

> A joint stool.

PETRUCHIO   **Thou** hast hit it. Come, sit on me.

KATHERINA

> Asses are made to bear, and so are **you**.

PETRUCHIO

> Women are made to bear, and so are **you**.

KATHERINA

> No such jade as **you**, if me **you** mean.

PETRUCHIO

> Alas, good Kate, I will not burden **thee**!

For knowing **thee** to be but young and light-

KATHERINA

Too light for such a swain as **you** to catch,
And yet as heavy as my weight should be.

PETRUCHIO

Should be? Should – buzz!

KATHERINA   Well ta'en, and like a buzzard.

PETRUCHIO

O slow-wing'd turtle, shall a buzzard take **thee**?

KATHERINA

Ay, for a turtle, as he takes a buzzard.

PETRUCHIO

Come, come **you** wasp; i'faith, **you** are too angry.

KATHERINA

If I be waspish, best beware my sting.

PETRUCHIO

My remedy is then to pluck it out.

KATHERINA

Ay, if the fool could find where it lies.

PETRUCHIO

Who knows not where a wasp does wear his sting?
In his tail.

KATHERINA In his tongue.

PETRUCHIO   Whose tongue?

KATHERINA

Yours, if **you** talk of tales, and so farewell.

PETRUCHIO

What, with my tongue in **your** tail? Nay, come again,
Good Kate. I am a gentleman –

KATHERINA   That I'll try.

She strikes him

PETRUCHIO

I swear I'll cuff **you**, if **you** strike again.

KATHERINA

So may **you** lose **your** arms.
If **you** strike me, **you** are no gentleman,
And if no gentleman, why then no arms.

PETRUCHIO

A herald, Kate? O, put me in **thy** books.

KATHERINA

What is **your** crest, a coxcomb?

PETRUCHIO

A combless cock, so Kate will be my hen.

KATHERINA

No cock of mine, **you** crow too like a craven.

PETRUCHIO

Nay, come, Kate, come; **you** must not look so sour.

KATHERINA

It is my fashion when I see a crab.

PETRUCHIO

Why, here's no crab, and therefore look not sour.

KATHERINA

There is, there is.

PETRUCHIO

Then show it me.

KATHERINA

Had I a glass, I would.

PETRUCHIO

What, **you** mean my face?

KATHERINA

Well aim'd of such a young one.

PETRUCHIO

Now, by Saint George, I am too young for **you**.

KATHERINA

Yet **you** are wither'd.

PETRUCHIO   'Tis with cares.

KATHERINA   I care not.

PETRUCHIO

Nay, hear **you** Kate – in sooth, **you** scape not so.

KATHERINA

I chafe **you**, if I tarry. Let me go.

PETRUCHIO

No, not a whit. I find **you** passing gentle.

'Twas told me **you** were rough, and coy, and sullen,

And now I find report a very liar;

For **thou** art pleasant, gamesome, passing courteous,

But slow in speech, yet sweet as springtime flowers.

Thou canst not frown, **thou** canst not look askance,

Nor bite the lip, as angry wenches will,

Nor hast **thou** pleasure to be cross in talk.

But **thou** with mildness entertain'st **thy** wooers,

With gentle conference, soft and affable.

Why does the world report that Kate doth limp?

O slanderous world! Kate like the hazel-twig

Is straight and slender, and as brown in hue

As hazel-nuts and sweeter than the kernels.

O, let me see **thee** walk. **Thou** dost not halt.

KATHERINA

Go, fool, and whom **thou** keep'st command.

PETRUCHIO

Did ever Dian so become a grove

As Kate this chamber with her princely gait?

O be **thou** Dian, and let her be Kate,

And then let Kate be chaste and Dian sportful.

KATHERINA

Where did **you** study all this goodly speech?

PETRUCHIO

It is extempore, from my mother-wit.

KATHERINA

A witty mother, witless else her son.

PETRUCHIO

Am I not wise?

KATHERINA   Yes, keep **you** warm.

PETRUCHIO

> Marry, so I mean, sweet Katherine, in **thy** bed.
> And therefore, setting all this chat aside,
> Thus in plain terms; **your** father hath consented
> That **you** shall be my wife; **your** dowry 'greed on:
> And will **you**, nill **you**, I will marry **you**.
> Now Kate, I am a husband for **your** turn,
> For by this light, whereby I see **thy** beauty,
> **Thy** beauty that doth make me like **thee** well,
> **Thou** must be married to no man but me.
> For I am he am born to tame **you**, Kate,
> And bring **you** from a wild Kate to a Kate
> Conformable as other household Kates.
> Here comes **your** father. Never make denial.
> I must and will have Katherine for my wife.

Petruchio's variations between **you** and **thou** are quite complex here. He starts with **you**, the appropriate address to someone he has never met before, but he quickly – and inappropriately – moves to **thou** when he starts on a conventional wooing speech that is obviously insincere and ironic. From then on, he uses **thou** when he is 'playing the lover' in an obviously false way and switches to **you** when they are trading insults and, at the end of the scene, when he lays on the line 'in plain terms' the reality of her situation: that her father has consented and 'will **you**, nill **you**, I will marry **you**'. He then repeats the **thou/you** pattern, using **thou** to talk about her beauty, but switching to **you** with, 'for I am born to tame **you**, Kate.' These switches are thoroughly disorienting for Katherina, who cannot know whether any of his wooing language is sincere. They put Petruchio in control of the scene's dynamics.

Katherina herself uses **thou** just once, in exasperation. She might be expected to use it more: transgressive women do use it more than more conventional ones. She is angry and is trying to assert herself, but Petruchio has established **thou** as the pronoun for his wooing, so she cannot use it back, as this would give their exchanges the pattern of dialogue between lovers – the mutual exchange of **thou**s. She would appear to collude in the pretence that this is a love scene. Already, at this stage in the play, Katherine is being disempowered by Petruchio – even her language choices are not her own.

Session three: Unwelcome advances

Exercise 1: *As You Like It* Act 3 Scene 5, 1–24.

Version One, in which both speakers use **you,** is perfectly possible. Silvius uses **you** because he is respectful to Phebe and he has not the confidence to use a lover's **thou** when she has already rejected him. And Phebe uses **you** to signal that she is cool and detached and has no wish to be closer to Silvius.

Version Two, in which both speakers use **thou,** would be very odd. **Thou** is too confident for Silvius's humble tone, and if Phebe uses **thou** too it becomes dialogue between lovers – the opposite of what she wants.

Version Three, in which Silvius uses **thou** and Phebe uses **you,** follows the pattern we saw in the previous session between Benedick and Beatrice and Petruchio and Katherina – the man woos with **thou** and the woman holds back with **you.** But Silvius does not have Petruchio's brash self-confidence, nor does he think, as Benedick does, that the woman he is wooing is secretly in love with him. He does not have the confidence for **thou**ing.

Version Four (below) is the correct version.

SILVIUS

    Sweet Phebe, do not scorn me, do not, Phebe.
    Say that **you** love me not but say not so
    In bitterness. The common executioner,
    Whose heart th'accustomed sight of death makes hard,
    Falls not the axe upon the humbled neck

But first begs pardon. Will **you** sterner be
Than he that dies and lives by bloody drops?

PHEBE

I would not be **thy** executioner.
I fly **thee** for I would not injure **thee**.
Thou tell'st me there is murder in mine eye:
'Tis pretty, sure, and very probable
That eyes, that are the frail'st and softest things,
That shut their coward gates on atomies,
Should be call'd tyrants, butchers, murderers!
Now I do frown on **thee** with all my heart
And if mine eyes can wound now let them kill **thee**.
Now counterfeit to swoon, why now fall down, –
Or if **thou** canst not, O for shame, for shame,
Lie not to say mine eyes are murderers!
Now show the wound mine eye hath made in **thee**.
Scratch **thee** but with a pin and there remains
Some scar of it. Lean but upon a rush,
The cicatrice and capable impressure
Thy palm some moment keeps; but now mine eyes
Which I have darted at **thee** hurt **thee** not,
Nor, I am sure, there is no power in eyes
That can do hurt.

SILVIUS   O dear Phebe,
If ever, as that ever may be near,
You find in some fresh cheek the power of fancy,
Then shall **you** see the wounds invisible
That love's keen arrow makes.

PHEBE   But till that time
Come not near me, and when that time comes

Afflict me with **thy** mocks, pity me not,
As till that time I shall not pity **thee**.

This version is, at first sight, surprising. Silvius's **you**s are unsurprising, as discussed above – he is being cautious and respectful – but why does Phebe use **thou** when she is rejecting Silvius? **Thou** can be used for anger and contempt, but Phebe's speeches are not angry. What is happening here is that Phebe is using the **thou**s of social patronage: she and Silvius are playing out a convention of the humble swain who is wooing the unattainable lady – Silvius is her servant, and that is how she addresses him, as his superior. It was a familiar literary convention when Shakespeare was writing. However, the actor playing Phebe, can use those **thou**s to good effect – not just being grand but exploiting the flirtatious connotations of **thou**. Looking at her language here, we can see how flirtatious it could be: 'Now I do frown on **thee**' can bring her quite close to him, and her talk of eyes – 'the frail'st and softest things', 'shutting their coward gates' suggests fluttering eyelashes. Then she talks of palms: does she show him her soft little palm? Or does she even take his palm? Given that, at the end of the play, she is happy to accept Silvius as her husband, an actor could suggest at this point that her rejection of him is, to some extent, a game that she is enjoying.

Exercise 2: *The Two Gentlemen of Verona* Act 5 Scene 4, 19–59.

Enter PROTEUS *and* SILVIA

PROTEUS

Madam, this service I have done for **you**
(Though **you** respect not aught **your** servant doth)
To hazard life, and rescue **you** from him
That would have forc'd **your** honour and **your** love.

Vouchsafe me for my meed but one fair look.

A smaller boon than this I cannot beg,

And less than this I am sure **you** cannot give.

SILVIA

O miserable, unhappy that I am!

PROTEUS

Unhappy were **you** madam, ere I came;

But by my coming I have made **you** happy.

SILVIA

By **thy** approach **thou** mak'st me most unhappy.

Had I been seized by a hungry lion,

I would have been a breakfast to the beast,

Rather than have false Proteus rescue me.

O heaven be judge how I love Valentine,

Whose life's as tender to me as my soul,

And full as much (for more there cannot be)

I do detest false perjur'd Proteus:

Therefore be gone, solicit me no more.

PROTEUS

What dangerous action, stood it next to death,

Would I not undergo for one calm look?

O 'tis the curse in love and still approved,

When women cannot love where they're belov'd.

SILVIA

When Proteus cannot love where he's belov'd

Read over Julia's heart, **thy** first best love,

For whose dear sake **thou** didst then rend **thy** faith

Into a thousand oaths; and all those oaths

Descended into perjury, to love me.

Thou hast no faith left now, unless **thou**'dst two,

And that's far worse than none: better have none

Than plural faith, which is too much by one.

Thou counterfeit to **thy** true friend!

PROTEUS

In love, who respects friend?

SILVIA   All men but Proteus

PROTEUS

Nay, if the gentle spirit of moving words

Can no way change **you** to a milder form,

I'll woo **you** like a soldier, at arms end,

And love **you** 'gainst the nature of love: force **you**.

SILVIA

O heaven!

PROTEUS   I'll force *thee* yield to my desire.

VALENTINE *(coming forward)*

Ruffian! Let go that rude uncivil touch,

Thou friend of an ill fashion!

Silvia, in this scene, is distraught and angry. She has lost her lover, has been frightened by outlaws and knows that Proteus is responsible for all her troubles, although he is trying to get credit for rescuing her. He is not using **thou** to her because he knows his advances are unwelcome and he is playing the gentleman, addressing her with respect. This allows Silvia to use contemptuous, angry **thou**s to him by contrast. If he had used **thou** to her, she could hardly have used it back to him, as this would have created a spurious impression of lovers' dialogue, using mutual **thou** in harmony with one another.

Proteus's one **thee** comes right at the end of the extract, when he threatens to rape her. He overtly abandons being a gentleman: 'Nay, if the gentle spirit of moving words/ Can in no way change **you**' and ends with 'I'll force **thee** yield to my desires'. It is not a lover's use; rather, it deliberately disrespects her and, at the same time, brings him close enough to take hold of her. Although the whole of his previous speech is threatening, he still uses **you** to her, cloaking the threat in acceptable language, talking of wooing her: 'I'll woo **you** like a soldier at arm's end. With 'I'll force **thee** yield to my desire', the switch to **thee** comes with the physical closeness that is actually an assault, an assault that provokes Valentine to come out of his hiding place and order him to 'let go that rude uncivil touch'. Shakespeare's texts, as printed in the First Folio of his works, have very few stage directions beyond entrances and exits. Later editors have added stage directions, but they are often unnecessary as the guide to the actors is in their lines. So, here, Proteus's move to take hold of Silvia is clearly signalled by his shift to '**thee**'.

Session four: Lèse-majesté

Exercise 1: *The Winter's Tale* Act 2 Scene3, 113–29 (abridged text).

LEONTES
I'll have **thee** burnt!

PAULINA   I care not
It is an heretic that makes the fire,
Not she that burns in't. I'll not call **you** tyrant;
But this most cruel usage of **your** queen –
Not able to produce more accusation
Than **your** own weak-hing'd fancy – something savours
Of tyranny and will ignoble make **you**,
Yea, scandalous to the world.

LEONTES   On **your** allegiance,
Out of the chamber with her!
[...]
                    Away with her!

PAULINA
I pray **you** do not push me; I'll be gone.
Look to **your** babe, my lord: 'tis **yours**. Jove send her
A better guiding spirit.
[...]
So, so: farewell; we are gone.

                    Exit

The Winter's Tale Act 3 Scene 2,173–99.

                    Enter PAULINA

PAULINA
What studied torments, tyrant, hast for me?

What wheels, racks, fires? What flaying, boiling
In leads or oils? What old or newer torture
Must I receive, whose every word deserves
To taste of **thy** most worse? **Thy** tyranny,
Together working with **thy** jealousies
(Fancies too weak for boys, too green and idle
For girls of nine), O think what they have done,
And then run mad indeed: stark mad! For all
Thy bygone fooleries were but spices of it.
That **thou** betray'dst Polixenes, 'twas nothing:
That did but show **thee**, of a fool, inconstant
And damnable ingrateful; nor was't much,
Thou would'st have poison'd good Camillo's honour,
To have him kill a king; poor trespasses,
More monstrous standing by: whereof I reckon
The casting forth to crows **thy** baby daughter,
To be none or little; though a devil
Would have shed water out of fire, ere done't:
Nor is't directly laid to **thee** the death
Of the young prince, whose honourable thoughts
(Thoughts high for one so tender) cleft the heart
That could conceive a gross and foolish sire
Blemish'd his gracious dam: this is not, no,
Laid to **thy** answer: but the last – O lords,
When I have said, cry 'woe!' – the queen, the queen,
The sweetest, dearest creature's dead; and vengeance for't
Not dropped down yet.

Paulina is furious even in the first scene, replying 'I care not' when
Leontes threatens to have her burnt as a witch, but she still uses **you**,
and she makes it clear that she is holding herself back from calling

him a tyrant, even though she is accusing him of tyrannous behaviour. She is still trying to get him to look at his own behaviour and see how he appears to the outside world, so she is restraining herself. When she returns in the second scene, she believes that her beloved mistress is dead and she gives full vent to her grief and her rage. She does not just switch to **thou** but uses it repeatedly, each **thou/thee/thy** acting like a physical blow against Leontes. In terms of movement, this brings her very close to Leontes, perhaps circling him, crowding him emotionally and overpowering him.

For an actor, these repeated **thou** forms should have a visceral effect. Even when actors do not recognise the significance of **thou** intellectually, they will often feel it physically: the forward 'th', formed by the tongue and the teeth, and the 'ou' vowel, again formed at the front of the mouth and shaped with the lips, are both more sensuous for expressing love and better designed for spitting rage than the more restrained **you**, starting at the back of the mouth and with tighter lips.

Exercise 2: *King Lear* Act 1 Scene 1, 145–90.

KENT   Royal Lear,
   Whom I have ever honoured as my king,
   Loved as my father, as my master followed,
   As my great patron thought on in my prayers –

LEAR
   The bow is bent and drawn; make from the shaft.

KENT
   Let it fall rather, though the fork invade
   The region of my heart: be Kent unmannerly
   When Lear is mad. What wouldst **thou** do, old man?

Think'st **thou** that duty shall have dread to speak,

When power to flattery bows? To plainness honour's bound

When majesty falls to folly. Reserve **thy** state,

And in **thy** best consideration check

This hideous rashness. Answer my life my judgement,

Thy youngest daughter does not love **thee** least,

Nor are those empty-hearted, whose low sounds

Reverb no hollowness.

LEAR   Kent, on **thy** life, no more.

KENT

My life I never held but as a pawn

To wage against **thine** enemies, ne'er fear to lose it,

Thy safety being the motive.

LEAR   Out of my sight!

KENT

See better, Lear, and let me still remain

The true blank of **thine** eye.

LEAR

Now by Apollo!

KENT   Now by Apollo, King,

Thou swear'st **thy** gods in vain.

LEAR   O vassal! Miscreant!

KENT

Do, kill **thy** physician, and **thy** fee bestow

Upon the foul disease. Revoke **thy** gift,

Or whilst I can vent clamour from my throat

I'll tell **thee, thou** dost evil.

LEAR

> Hear me, recreant, on **thine** allegiance, hear me:
> That **thou** hast sought to make us break our vows,
> Which we durst never yet, and with strained pride
> To come betwixt our sentences and our power,
> Which nor our nature, nor our place can bear,
> Our potency made good, take **thy** reward.
> Five days do we allot **thee** for provision,
> To shield **thee** from disasters of the world,
> And on the sixth to turn **thy** hated back
> Upon our kingdom. If on the next day following
> **Thy** banished trunk be found in our dominions,
> The moment is **thy** death. Away, By Jupiter,
> This shall not be revoked.

KENT

> Why, fare **thee** well, King, since thus **thou** wilt appear,
> Freedom lives hence and banishment is here.
> (*to* CORDELIA) The gods to their dear shelter take **thee**, maid,
> That justly think'st and hast most rightly said;
> (*to* GONERIL *and* REGAN) And **your** large speeches may **your**
>   deeds approve,
> That good effects may spring from words of love.
> Thus Kent, O Princes, bids **you** all adieu;
> He'll shape his old course in a country new.

As you see, all the pronouns are **thou** forms here, from both speakers. Kent is horrified by the king's behaviour and is, perhaps, trying to shock him out of his madness, as he sees it. He starts very respectfully but then seems to make a decision to break all the rules. He actually prepares the way for this when he says, 'Be Kent unmannerly when Lear is mad'. He intends to be 'unmannerly'. He addresses the king as 'old man', and with that kind of disrespect the only possible pronoun is **thou**. Once he has started **thou**ing, he carries on, addressing Lear as 'King' rather than '**Your** Majesty'. Lear responds in kind. To use **you** in response to Kent's **thou**s would be to reverse the status relationship between them, and, anyway, Lear is in the kind of rage which is usually expressed with **thou**. So, the two of them battle each other with furious, emotional **thou**s, but Lear asserts the status difference between them by using the royal **we** of himself. On Kent's side those **thou**s can also express his deep love for and loyalty to his king. As he leaves, Kent also uses affectionate **thee** to Cordelia – a reminder that he has known her since she was a child. The whole scene is given an additional emotional charge and a sense of danger by the use of **thou**.

Exercise 3: *Measure for Measure* Act 2 Scene 4, 140–60.

Here is the authentic version of this exchange.

ANGELO

Plainly conceive, I love **you**.

ISABELLA

My brother did love Juliet,
And **you** tell me that he shall die for't.

ANGELO

He shall not, Isabel, if **you** give me love.

ISABELLA

I know **your** virtue hath a licence in't
Which seems a little fouler than it is,
To pluck on others.

ANGELO   Believe me, on mine honour,

My words express my purpose.

ISABELLA

Ha? Little honour, to be much believ'd,

And most pernicious purpose! Seeming, seeming!

I will proclaim **thee**, Angelo, look for't.

Sign me a present pardon for my brother,

Or with an outstretch'd throat I'll tell the world aloud

What man **thou** art.

ANGELO   Who will believe **thee**, Isabel?

My unsoil'd name, th'austereness of my life,

My vouch against **you**, and my place i'th' state

Will so **your** accusation overweigh,

That **you** shall stifle in **your** own report,

And smell of calumny. I have begun

And now I give my sensual race the rein:

Fit **thy** consent to my sharp appetite;

Lay by all nicety and prolixious blushes

That banish what they sue for. Redeem **thy** brother

By yielding up **thy** body to my will;

Or else he must not only die the death,

But **thy** unkindness shall his death draw out

To lingering sufferance. Answer me tomorrow,

Or by the affection that now guides me most,

I'll prove a tyrant to him. As for **you**,

Say what **you** can: my false o'erweighs **your** true.

Angelo and Isabella are both using **you** initially, as we would expect: Isabella uses it respectfully to the Duke's Deputy (notice that she calls him 'gentle my lord') and Angelo uses it formally as to a woman who has come to see him on government business. The moment of truth for Isabella comes when she realizes that Angelo is offering to spare Claudio if she will give in to his sexual demands. 'I will proclaim **thee** Angelo' is a cry of pure outrage, and now he is no longer 'my lord' but plain 'Angelo'. 'What man **thou** art' reflects this too: she will tell the world about the corrupt man inside the outward dignity of the Duke's Deputy. Angelo flashes back in retaliation, 'Who will believe **thee** Isabel?' echoing her '**thee**' and the use of the bare forename. He returns to **you** to maintain his role as Deputy and to emphasize how much more credible he is than her. But now they are open antagonists and as he starts to threaten her, he switches to **thou** again, suggesting that he gets closer to her to intimidate her physically. Finally, he reverts to **you** to dismiss her with his cynical summing up – 'my false o'erweighs **your** true'.

Session five: Family values

Exercise 1: *Hamlet* Act 1 Scene 2, 42–75 (abridged text).

KING

>And now, Laertes, what's the news with **you**?
>**You** told us of some suit: what is't Laertes?
>**You** cannot speak of reason to the Dane
>And lose **your** voice. What wouldst **thou** beg, Laertes,
>That shall not be my offer, not **thy** asking?
>The head is not more native to the heart,
>The hand more instrumental to the mouth,
>Than is the throne of Denmark to **thy** father.
>What wouldst **thou** have Laertes?

LAERTES   My dread lord,

>**Your** leave and favour to return to France,
>From whence though willingly I came to Denmark
>To show my duty in **your** coronation,
>Yet now I must confess, that duty done,
>My thoughts and wishes bend again toward France
>And bow them to **your** gracious leave and pardon.

KING

>Have **you your** father's leave? What says Polonius?

POLONIUS

>He hath, my lord, wrung from me my slow leave
>By laboursome petition, and at last
>Upon his will I seal'd my hard consent.
>I do beseech **you** give him leave to go.

KING

> Take **thy** fair hour, Laertes, time be **thine**,
> And **thy** best graces spend it at **thy** will.
> But now, my cousin Hamlet, and my son –

HAMLET

> A little more than kin, and less than kind.

KING

> How is it that the clouds still hang on **you**?

HAMLET

> Not so, my lord, I am too much in the sun.

QUEEN

> Good Hamlet, cast **thy** knighted colour off,
> And let **thine** eye look like a friend on Denmark.
> Do not for ever with **thy** vailed lids
> Seek for **thy** noble father in the dust.
> **Thou** know'st 'tis common: all that lives, must die,
> Passing through nature to eternity.

HAMLET

> Ay, madam, it is common.

QUEEN   If it be,
> Why seems it so particular with **thee**?

HAMLET

> Seems, madam? Nay, it is. I know not 'seems'.
> 'Tis not alone my inky cloak, good mother,
> Nor customary suits of solemn black
> That can denote me truly. These indeed seem,
> But I have that within which passes show,
> These but the trappings and the suits of woe.

KING

    'Tis sweet and commendable in **your** nature, Hamlet,

    To give these mourning duties to **your** father,

    But **you** must know **your** father lost a father,

    That father lost, lost his, and the survivor bound

    In filial obligation for some term

    To do obsequious sorrow. But to persever

    In obstinate condolement is a course

    Of impious stubbornness, 'tis unmanly grief.

    [...]

                We pray **you** throw to earth

    This unprevailing woe, and think of us

    As of a father; for let the world take note

    You are the most immediate to our throne,

    And with no less nobility of love

    Than that which dearest father bears his son

    Do I impart toward **you**. For **your** intent

    In going back to school in Wittenberg

    It is most retrograde to our desire,

    And we beseech **you** bend **you** to remain

    Here in the cheer and comfort of our eye,

    Our chiefest courtier, cousin and our son.

QUEEN

    Let not **thy** mother lose her prayers, Hamlet.

    I pray **thee** stay with us. Go not to Wittenberg.

HAMLET

    I shall in all my best obey **you**, madam.

For King Claudius this is a crucially important occasion. He has to establish himself as king and overcome possible objections to his marrying his dead brother's wife. He must obviously take centre stage here, establishing his authority. His opening words to Laertes perhaps invite him to approach, and then, when Laertes is quite close, he starts to address him with **thou**. This can be seen as a patronizing use by a king to a subject, but Claudius's words are brimming with kindness both towards Laertes and to his father, so it does seem to be an affectionate use, too. If Polonius has been at court for a long time, perhaps Claudius has known Laertes since he was a boy. Polonius is going to be important to Claudius in governing the country, so showing favour to Laertes may also be seen as a way of securing Polonius's loyalty. When he grants Laertes' request to return to France, with 'Take **thy** fair hour', he is likely to be close to him – might perhaps put a hand on his shoulder.

This kindly **thou**ing contrasts with the **you** he gives Hamlet – even though he calls him his cousin and his son. Later in the scene, he refuses Hamlet permission to return to his studies, so a contrast is set up between his attitude to the two young men. His question to Hamlet, 'How is it that the clouds still hang on **you**?', refers to the fact that Hamlet alone is still wearing mourning black for his father while the rest of the court is in wedding finery. We can see that Hamlet is an irritant to Claudius, spoiling his performance in his new role as king. Hamlet needs to be on the edge of the scene, downstage where he can make his aside to the audience, 'A little more than kin and less than kind'. We can see now that Claudius can have been playing up his kindness to Laertes for Hamlet's benefit, demonstrating how generous he can be to a young man who behaves well.

Gertrude intervenes between Claudius and Hamlet, using **thou** to him. She needs to move close to Hamlet, physically breaking the eyeline between Claudius and him.. Here she may be wanting to compensate for Claudius's coldness of tone, but in fact she uses **thou** to Hamlet throughout the play, repeatedly calling him 'my son'. She knows that she has upset him deeply by marrying his uncle so soon after his father's death, and she needs to keep reassuring him of her love for him. We might also feel that in using **thou** to him she is treating him as a boy, rather than the man he is, this justifying Claudius's seizure of the throne.

Exercise 2: *Hamlet* Act 1 Scene 3, 55–136 (abridged text).

Enter POLONIUS

POLONIUS

> Yet here, Laertes? Aboard, aboard for shame.
> The wind sits in the shoulder of **your** sail
> And **you** are stay'd for. There, my blessing with **thee**.
> And these few precepts in **thy** memory
> Look **thou** character. Give **thy** thoughts no tongue,
> Nor any unproportion'd thought his act.
> Be **thou** familiar, but by no means vulgar;
> Those friends **thou** hast, and their adoption tried,
> Grapple them unto **thy** soul with hoops of steel.
> Give every man **thy** ear, but few **thy** voice;
> Neither a borrower nor a lender be,
> For loan oft loses both itself and friend.
> This above all, to **thine** own self be true,
> And it must follow as the night the day
> **Thou** canst not then be false to any man.
> Farewell, my blessing season this in **thee**.

LAERTES

> Most humbly do I take my leave, my lord.

POLONIUS

> The time invests **you**; go, **your** servants tend.

LAERTES

    Farewell, Ophelia, and remember well

    What I have said to **you**.

OPHELIA   'Tis in my memory lock'd,

    And **you** alone shall keep the key of it.

LAERTES

    Farewell.

Exit

POLONIUS

    What is't, Ophelia, he hath said to **you**?

OPHELIA

    So please **you**, something touching the Lord Hamlet.

POLONIUS

    Marry, well bethought.

    'Tis told me he hath very oft of late

    Given private time to **you**, and **you yourself**

    Have of **your** audience been most free and bounteous.

    If it be so – and so 'tis put on me,

    And that in way of caution – I must tell **you**

    You do not understand **yourself** so clearly

    As it behoves my daughter and **your** honour.

    What is between **you**? Give me up the truth.

OPHELIA

    He hath, my lord, of late made many tenders

    Of his affection to me.

POLONIUS

    Affection? Pooh, **you** speak like a green girl,

Unsifted in such perilous circumstance.
Do **you** believe his tenders, as **you** call them?

OPHELIA

I do not know, my lord, what I should think.

POLONIUS

Marry, I will teach **you**, think **yourself** a baby
That **you** have ta'en these tenders for true pay
Which are not sterling. Tender **yourself** more dearly.
Or **you'll** tender me a fool.

OPHELIA

My lord, he hath importuned me with love
In honourable fashion.

POLONIUS

Ay, fashion **you** may call it. Go to, go to.

OPHELIA

And hath given countenance to his speech, my lord,
With almost all the holy vows of heaven.

POLONIUS

Ay, springes to catch woodcocks. I do know
When the blood burns, how prodigal the soul
Lends the tongue vows.
[...]
                          This is for all,
I would not, in plain terms, from this time forth
Have **you** so slander any moment leisure
As to give words or talk with the Lord Hamlet.
Look to't I charge **you**. Come **your** ways.

OPHELIA

I shall obey, my lord.

Exeunt

If a parent uses **thou** to one child and **you** to another, there is a significant difference in the relationships s/he has with the two of them, or a significant difference in the context in which the dialogue takes place. In the case of Polonius, the context appears superficially to be the same – he is giving each of his children advice about how to behave – but there is a difference in the tone of his advice: to Laertes Polonius is giving general 'precepts', without any suggestion that he thinks he has been, or will be, behaving badly; with Ophelia, he is already concerned about the way she has been accepting Hamlet's attentions, and is worried about her apparent naiveté, afraid that she will let Hamlet seduce her and dishonour the family. So, his **thou**s to Laertes may feel appropriate for an affectionate father dispensing parental advice, while his **you**s to Ophelia are more distant because he is worried and irritated – though not annoyed enough to **thou** her in anger. However, look at Polonius's third line:

And **you** are stay'd for. There, my blessing with **thee**.

'There', together with the switch to **thee**, is a clear direction to the actor that he embraces Laertes – or even kisses him. Ophelia never gets that kind of affection from her father. And there is other evidence in the play that Polonius may have more affection for his son than for his daughter. He tells the king, in the previous scene, that Laertes has 'wrung' from him his 'slow leave' to go back to Paris – he was reluctant to let him go away again. He never really engages affectionately with Ophelia, however. When she runs to him in fright because she has had a strange and alarming visit from Hamlet, he makes no effort to comfort her, but is concerned only with Hamlet's state of mind and its implications for the king. Later, when he and the king use Ophelia as a decoy so that they can eavesdrop on Hamlet talking with her, Hamlet treats her so harshly that she is left in tears, but Polonius, emerging from his hiding place, simply dismisses her with, 'You need not tell us what the matter is/ We heard it all' – hardly the attitude of an affectionate father. Ophelia has lost Hamlet's love and has no-one to turn to for comfort.

After Polonius is killed by Hamlet, Laertes returns from Paris to raise a protest, demanding justice for his father's death – a conventional response by a loving son. Ophelia has a mental breakdown, talking constantly of seduced and abandoned girls, and of her father's death. She has been abandoned twice – by Hamlet and by her father – but perhaps her grief at her father's death can be seen not simply as grief at the loss of a loving father and protector but partly as grief that she will never now feel her father's love.

Session six: Married love

Exercise 1: *Macbeth* Act 1 Scene 7, 28–62.

Enter LADY MACBETH

MACBETH

How now! What news?

LADY MACBETH

He hath almost supp'd. Why have **you** left the chamber?

MACBETH

Hath he ask'd for me?

LADY MACBETH   Know **you** not he hath?

MACBETH

We will proceed no further in this business.
He hath honoured me of late; and I have bought
Golden opinions from all sorts of people,
Which would be worn now in their newest gloss,
Not cast aside so soon.

LADY MACBETH   Was the hope drunk
Wherein **you** dress'd **yourself**? Hath it slept since?
And wakes it now to look so green and pale
At what it did so freely? From this time
Such I account **thy** love. Art **thou** afear'd
To be the same in **thine** own act and valour
As **thou** art in desire? Would'st **thou** have that
Which **thou** esteem'st the ornament of life,
And live a coward in **thine** own esteem,
Letting 'I dare not' wait upon 'I would',
Like the poor cat i'th' adage?

MACBETH **Prithee**, peace!
I dare do all that may become a man;
Who dares do more is none.

LADY MACBETH What beast was't then
That made **you** break this enterprise to me?
When **you** durst do it then **you** were a man:
And to be more than what **you** were, **you** would
Be so much more the man. Nor time nor place
Did then adhere, and yet **you** would make both:
They have made themselves, and that their fitness now
Hath unmade **you**. I have given suck, and know
How tender 'tis to love the babe that milks me:
I would, while it was smiling in my face,
Have pluck'd my nipple from his boneless gums,
And dash'd the brains out, had I so sworn
As **you** have done to this.

MACBETH If we should fail?

LADY MACBETH We fail!
But screw **your** courage to the sticking place
And we'll not fail. When Duncan is asleep
(Whereto the rather his day's hard journey
Shall soundly invite him) his two chamberlains
Will I with wine and wassail so convince
That memory, the warder of the brain,
Shall be a fume. When in swinish sleep
Their drenched natures lie, as in a death,
What cannot **you** and I perform
Upon the unguarded Duncan? What not put upon
His spongy officers, who shall bear the guilt
Of our great quell?

MACBETH   Bring forth men children only!
  For **thy** undaunted mettle should compose
  Nothing but males!
  I am settled and bend up
  Each corporal agent to this terrible feat.
  Away, and mock the time with fairest show:
  False face must hide what the false heart doth know.

Lady Macbeth starts with neutral **you** to her husband and after he drops the bombshell, 'We will proceed no further with this business' she does not immediately react with angry **thou**s, but builds up momentum and then uses **thou** in a speech that condemns Scotland's greatest general as 'a coward', 'afear'd', 'crying "I dare not"'. It is a reckless thing to call a soldier a coward, and Macbeth comes back strongly in his own defence. If Lady Macbeth's **thou**s bring her close to her husband, then his response could be physically threatening to her, a reason for her to switch to less aggressive **you**s. Even if she is not threatened by him, she does decide on a change of tack. Having knocked him down with taunts of cowardice, she starts to build him up again with a picture of what a great man he can be, and the **you**s she addresses him with give him respect. This seems, in fact, to be the strategy she adopts for the rest of the play: she does not risk using **thou** contemptuously to him again, even when he goes to pieces after he has murdered Duncan, or later when he sees the ghost of murdered Banquo and is gibbering with fear. And from the moment he becomes king she addresses him as 'my lord'. But this also puts a distance between them. Macbeth told her she would be his 'dearest partner in greatness' but we see them become more and more distant from one another.

Macbeth says '**prithee** peace' to her when he is angrily fending off her accusations of cowardice and then has one significant '**thy**', when he succumbs to her arguments, in a burst of admiration at her courage and determination:

> Bring forth men children only
> For **thy** undaunted mettle should compose
> Nothing but males.

'Thy' expresses his love and admiration for the partner with whom he hopes to have children. We can also see him as addressing her as a comrade in arms – soldiers often use **thou** to each other.

Exercise 2: *Henry IV Part One* Act 2 Scene 3, 73–117.

In the text below, names and titles that are at odds with the pronouns used are in italics.

LADY PERCY
> Tell me, sweet *lord*, what is't that takes from **thee**
> **Thy** stomach, pleasure and **thy** golden sleep?
> Some heavy business hath my lord in hand,
> And I must know it, else he loves me not.

HOTSPUR
> What ho!

Enter a SERVANT
> Is Gilliams with the packet gone?

SERVANT
> He is, my lord, an hour ago.

HOTSPUR
> Bid Butler lead my horse into the park.

Exit SERVANT

LADY PERCY

But hear **you**, my lord.

HOTSPUR

What say'st **thou**, *my lady*?

LADY PERCY

What is it carries **you** away?

HOTSPUR

Why, my horse, my love, my horse.

LADY PERCY

Out, **you** *mad-headed ape!*
A weasel hath not such a deal of spleen
As **you** are toss'd with. In faith,
I'll know **your** business, *Harry*, that I will;
I fear my brother Mortimer doth stir
About his title, and hath sent for **you**
To line his enterprise. But if **you** go –

HOTSPUR

So far afoot I shall be weary, love.

LADY PERCY

Come, come, **you** *paraquito*, answer me
Directly unto this question that I ask.
In faith, I'll break **thy** little finger, Harry.
And if **thou** wilt not tell me all things true.

HOTSPUR

Away, away, **you** *trifler*! Love! I love **thee** not,

I care not for **thee**, Kate; this is no world
To play with mammets, and to tilt with lips;
We must have bloody noses and crack'd crowns.
What say'st **thou**, Kate? What would'st **thou** have with me?

LADY PERCY

Do **you** not love me? Do **you** not indeed?
Well, do not then, for since **you** love me not
I will not love myself. Do **you** not love me?
Nay, tell me if **you** speak in jest or no.

HOTSPUR

Come, wilt **thou** see me ride?
And when I am a horseback I will swear
I love **thee** infinitely. But hark **you** *Kate*,
I must not have **you** henceforth question me
Whither I go, nor reason whereabout:
Whither I must I must; and, to conclude,
This evening must I leave **you** *gentle Kate*.
I know **you** wise, but yet no farther wise
Than Harry Percy's wife; constant **you** are,
But yet a woman, and for secrecy
No lady closer, for I well believe
Thou wilt not utter what **thou** dost not know;
And so far will I trust **thee**, gentle Kate.

LADY PERCY

How? So far?

HOTSPUR

Not an inch further. But hear **you**, *Kate*,
Whither I go, thither shall **you** go too:

Today will I set forth, tomorrow **you.**
Will that content **you,** *Kate?*

LADY PERCY
It must, of force.

Exeunt

Hotspur and his wife are clearly conflicted in their feelings for one another in this scene. Lady Percy loves her husband but is worried about what he is planning and angry with him for shutting her out and not trusting her enough to tell her his plans. Hotspur loves his wife but is distracted by his plans, needs to keep them secret even from her and, most importantly, he cannot afford to let his love for her make him soft – this is a time for 'bloody noses' and 'crack'd crowns'. The ambivalence of their feelings is made very clear by the way the names they call each other so often contrast with the pronouns they use.

Hotspur starts it, when Lady Percy calls him 'my lord', and he echoes her with 'my lady' but changes the pronoun to more affectionate **thou** – a very unusual combination. Then Lady Percy throws insults at him, calling him a 'paraquito' and a 'mad-headed ape', but not using the **thou**s that usually go with those sorts of insults; it seems that she is frustrated and angry but still doesn't want to use **thou** contemptuously because it is the pronoun of affection between them. It is only when she threatens him – 'I'll break **thy** little finger Harry' – that she **thou**s him, and then, of course, she has to be very close to him physically, probably seizing his hand. Hotspur shakes her off physically and tries to shake her off emotionally – 'I love **thee** not', 'I care not for **thee,** Kate', but his **thou**s are a give-away – in saying that he does not love her, he uses the lover's pronoun. And he continues to use mainly **thou** to her until he switches into practical mode, giving her instructions and telling her that he is leaving. Then **you** is his businesslike pronoun, avoiding the emotional entanglements of **thou**.

We see the dynamic and complex relationship of a couple who are in love but are wrestling with a situation that tests their love to its limits.

Session seven: Freudian slips and testing moments

Exercise 1

Love's Labour's Lost Act 2 Scene 1.
As You Like It Act 5 Scene 2.
Romeo and Juliet Act 3 Scene 5.

Love's Labour's Lost Act 2 Scene 1, 168–78.

KING

> Meantime, receive such welcome at my hand
> As honour, without breach of honour, may
> Make tender of to **thy** true worthiness.
> **You** may not come, fair Princess, within my gates,
> But here without **you** shall be so received
> As **you** shall deem **yourself** lodged in my heart,
> Though so denied fair harbour in my house.
> **Your** own good thoughts excuse me, and farewell.
> Tomorrow we shall visit **you** again.

PRINCESS

> Sweet health and fair desires consort **your** grace.

KING

> **Thy** own wish wish I **thee** in every place.

The King is in a very difficult situation here: his vow means that he cannot offer the Princess the hospitality that her position demands, and he has the embarrassing task of negotiating with a woman and telling her that her father is a cheat and a liar! For the most part, he maintains formal, respectful **you**. What his slips into **thou** tell us is that he is also falling in love with her. Boyet, the Queen's Chamberlain, comments afterwards that 'Navarre is infected' (with love). In his long speech, the King uses several 'wooing' phrases that might be regarded simply as chivalrous – an attempt to compensate for his poor hospitality: 'fair princess', 'as **you** shall deem **yourself** lodged in my heart'. The slips into **thou** forms are what tell us that the king is expressing more than mere chivalry. Might he kiss her hand in his farewell speech? This could be regarded as no more than a courtesy, but can also express more.

As You Like It Act 5 Scene 2, 19–27.

ROSALIND

O my dear Orlando, how it grieves me to see **thee** wear **thy** heart in a scarf!

ORLANDO

It is my arm.

ROSALIND

I thought **thy** heart had been wounded with the claws of a lion.

ORLANDO

Wounded it is but with the eyes of a lady.

ROSALIND

Did **your** brother tell **you** how I counterfeited to swoon when he showed me **your** handkerchief?

ORLANDO

Ay, and greater wonders than that.

Rosalind's persona as Ganymede is beginning to unravel. Her feelings for Orlando are becoming more obvious and she is finding it increasingly difficult to hide them. The shock of seeing Orlando after he has been mauled by a lion makes her slip into **thou**. She recovers herself and starts to use **you** as usual but the slip has reminded her of her earlier 'slip', when she fainted in a stereotypically female way. She knows that she is beginning to give herself away and tries to make an excuse for herself by claiming that she 'feigned' to swoon. In her mind, her **thou**ing and her fainting are connected and she is trying to excuse both of them. (In some productions there is a suggestion that Orlando's brother, Oliver, realizes that 'Ganymede' is female when he picks her up after she faints, and has told Orlando of his suspicions, so Orlando's line, 'Ay, and greater wonders than that' is said with that implication. You might like to try giving the scene that slant.)

Romeo and Juliet Act 3 Scene 5, 48–59.

ROMEO

> Farewell.
> I will omit no opportunity
> That may convey my greetings, love, to **thee**.

JULIET

> O think'st **thou** we shall ever meet again?

ROMEO

> I doubt it not, and all these woes shall serve
> For sweet discourses in our times to come.

JULIET

> O God, I have an ill-divining soul.
> Methinks I see **thee** now **thou** art below
> As one dead in the bottom of a tomb.
> Either my eyesight fails or **thou** look'st pale.

ROMEO

> And trust me, love, in my eyes so do **you**.
> Dry sorrow drinks our blood. Adieu, adieu.

Exit

Romeo's last couplet, with its odd '**you**', are the last words that Juliet hears him say to her. They could be explained simply by the rhyme with 'adieu'; rhyming couplets like this often come at the end of a scene and they also sometimes mark significant exits. It seems unlikely, though, that Shakespeare would have put **you** into Romeo's mouth at this crucial point simply because it gave him an easy rhyme. It is perhaps more likely that we see the nearness/distance aspect of **thou** and **you** here; the lovers are being physically pulled apart at this point, disappearing from one another, seeing each other as pale ghosts. Romeo's sad '**you**' can reflect this.

Exercise 2

Hamlet Act 3 Scene 1.
Othello Act 3 Scene 4.
Midsummer Night's Dream Act 2 Scene 1.

Hamlet Act 3 Scene 1, 121–38.

HAMLET

Get **thee** to a nunnery. Why wouldst **thou** be a breeder of sinners? I am myself indifferent honest, but yet I could accuse me of such things that it were better my mother had not borne me. I am very proud, revengeful, ambitious, with more offences at my beck than I have thoughts to put them in, imagination to give them shape, or time to act them in. What should such fellows as I do crawling between earth and heaven? We are arrant knaves all, believe none of us. Go **thy** ways to a nunnery. Where's *your* father?

OPHELIA
At home, my lord.

HAMLET

Let the doors be shut upon him, that he may play the fool nowhere but in's own house. Farewell.

OPHELIA

O help him, **you** sweet heavens.

HAMLET

If **thou** dost marry, I'll give **thee** this plague for **thy** dowry; be **thou** as chaste as ice, as pure as snow, **thou** shalt not escape calumny. Get **thee** to a nunnery. Farewell.

Hamlet is in a highly emotional state in this scene, and his **thou**ing of Ophelia seems to express a combination of anger and distress. **Thou** is always a marker of heightened emotion. As the text above shows, his switch to **you** comes when he asks Ophelia where her father is. Productions vary in the way this is played. In some productions, he has not realized until then that they are being spied on. In others, he has known from the start and is partly putting on a performance for the listeners. In this case, the question, 'Where is **your** father?' is a test of her honesty – a test which she fails because she lies to him. Bear in mind, when staging the scene, that **your** takes Hamlet away physically from Ophelia.

Othello Act 3 Scene 4, 32–57 (abridged text).

OTHELLO

How do **you**, Desdemona?

DESDEMONA   Well, my good lord.

OTHELLO

Give me **your** hand. This hand is moist, my lady.

DESDEMONA

It hath felt no age, nor known no sorrow.

OTHELLO

[. . .]

'Tis a good hand,

A frank one.

DESDEMONA   **You** may indeed say so,

For 'twas that hand that gave away my heart.

Come now, **your** promise.

OTHELLO

What promise, chuck?

DESDEMONA

I have sent to bid Cassio come speak with **you**.

OTHELLO

I have a salt and sullen rheum offends me.

Lend me *thy* handkerchief.

DESDEMONA   Here, my lord.

OTHELLO

That which I gave **you**.

DESDEMONA   I have it not about me.

OTHELLO

Not?

DESDEMONA   No, faith, my lord.

OTHELLO

That's a fault.

Earlier in the play, Othello uses **thou** affectionately to Desdemona, but now Iago has made her suspicious of her he is using **you**. Iago has planted in his mind the idea that Desdemona has given Cassio her handkerchief and at the point where Othello asks for the handkerchief he switches to **thy**. Either he is trying to wrongfoot her by switching to the intimate pronoun – a husband casually asking his wife if he can borrow her hanky to wipe his nose – or he actually hopes that all can be well, that she will produce the handkerchief and it really will be a domestic moment. Either way, the **thy** brings him close to her – threatening or appealing. Notice that he switches immediately back to **you** – 'That which I gave **you**'. If he is simply trying to catch her out, then that **you** becomes a challenge; if he is hoping that she has the handkerchief then the **you** can express disappointment and withdrawal.

A Midsummer Night's Dream Act 2 Scene 1, 118–45 (abridged text).

OBERON

> Do **you** amend it then: it lies in **you**.
> Why should Titania cross her Oberon?
> I do but beg a little changeling boy
> To be my henchman.

TITANIA   Set **your** heart at rest.
> The fairy land buys not the child of me
> His mother was a votaress of my order
> [. . .]
> But she, being mortal, of that child did die,
> And for her sake do I rear up her boy,
> And for her sake I will not part with him.

OBERON

> How long within this wood intend **you** stay?

TITANIA

> Perchance till after Theseus' wedding day.
> If **you** will patiently dance in our round,
> And see our moonlight revels, go with us;
> If not, shun me, and I will spare **your** haunts.

OBERON

> Give me that boy, and I will go with *thee*.

TITANIA

> Not for *thy* fairy kingdom. Fairies, away.
> We shall chide downright if I longer stay.

Exeunt TITANIA *and her train*

Oberon has used **thou** aggressively earlier in the scene, and Titania has used it back to him. In the extract above they have cooled down to **you** but Oberon suddenly switches to **thee** to wheedle her, to offer peace if she will just give him the boy. It looks as though he thinks he can slip in his 'deal' as a small request between husband and wife, but Titania responds aggressively, using **thy** back to him. Again 'I will go with **thee**' should bring Oberon close to Titania, and this gives her the opportunity to snap 'Not for **thy** fairy kingdom' into his face before she turns away. As often, the pronoun switches offer stage directions.

Session eight: Absent friends

Julius Caesar Act 3 Scene 1 (Mark Antony).

Julius Caesar Act 3 Scene 1 (Mark Antony).

King Lear Act 4 Scene 7 (Cordelia).

Macbeth Act 3 Scene 1 (Banquo).

Much Ado About Nothing Act 3 Scene 1 (Beatrice).

Exercise 1

Julius Caesar Act 3 Scene 1, 185–203 (abridged text).

ANTONY

    First, Marcus Brutus, will I shake with **you**.

    Next, Caius Cassius, do I take **your** hand.

    Now, Decius Brutus, **yours**. Now **yours**, Metellus.

    Yours, Cinna, and my valiant Casca, **yours**.

    Though last, not least in love, **yours** good Trebonius.

    Gentlemen all; alas, what shall I say?

    My credit now stands on such slippery ground

    That one of two bad ways **you** must conceit me,

    Either a coward or a flatterer.

    That I did love **thee**, Caesar, O 'tis true:

    If then **thy** spirit look upon us now,

    Shall it not grieve **thee** dearer than **thy** death

    To see **thy** Antony making his peace,

    Shaking the bloody fingers of **thy** foes,

    Most noble in the presence of **thy** corpse.

    Had I as many eyes as **thou** hast wounds

    Weeping as fast as they stream forth **thy** blood,

    It would become me better than to close

    In terms of friendship with **thine** enemies.

Julius Caesar Act 3 Scene 1, 254–75 (abridged text).

ANTONY

> O pardon me, **thou** bleeding piece of earth,
> That I am meek and gentle with these butchers.
> **Thou** art the ruins of the noblest man
> That ever lived in the tide of times.
> Woe to the hand that shed this costly blood.
> Over **thy** wounds now I do prophesy,
> A curse shall light upon the limbs of men:
> Domestic fury and fierce civil strife
> Shall cumber all the parts of Italy;
> [. . .]
> And Caesar's spirit, ranging for revenge,
> With Ate by his side, come hot from hell,
> Shall in these confines, with a monarch's voice,
> Cry havoc, and let slip the dogs of war.

In the first speech, there is, of course, a marked contrast between Antony's **you**s to Caesar's murderers, as he shakes hands with them, and his **thou**s to the dead Caesar. His move to **thou** when he speaks to Caesar's body is dictated by the convention that **thou** is used to the dead (addressing Caesar as **thou** bleeding piece of earth highlights the fact that Caesar is no longer a person). But his **thou**ing also allows Antony to express his heartfelt grief for Caesar, and it emphasizes the insincerity of his 'pact' with his killers. In the first extract, the killers are listening, so Antony can only express his grief, but not his anger. In the second speech, when Antony is left alone with Caesar's body, the **thou**s help him to express his rage and his furious determination to avenge Caesar's death. The conventional **thou** use goes alongside the general pattern that **thou** becomes more frequent with a rising emotional temperature.

King Lear Act 4 Scene 7, 26–44 (abridged text).

CORDELIA

> O my dear father, restoration hang
> **Thy** medicine on my lips, and let this kiss
> Repair those violent harms that my two sisters
> Have in **thy** reverence made.
> [...]
>
> and wast **thou** fain, poor father,
> To hovel **thee** with swine and rogues forlorn
> In short and musty straw? Alack, alack!
> 'Tis wonder that **thy** life and wits at once
> Had not concluded all. He wakes.
> How does my royal lord? How fares **your** majesty?

Cordelia would never normally address her father with **thou** and we see how, as soon as he wakes, she calls him '**your** majesty', but when he is sleeping **thou** is appropriate and allows Cordelia to express her pity and tenderness for her father, so that, in that moment, their roles are almost reversed, and she speaks like a mother over her sleeping child.

Macbeth Act 3 Scene 1, 1–18

BANQUO

> **Thou** hast it now, King, Cawdor, Glamis, all,
> As the weird women promis'd; and, I fear,
> **Thou** play'dst most foully for't; yet it was said
> It should not stand in **thy** posterity;
> But that myself should be the root and father
> Of many kings. If there come truth from them
> (As upon **thee**, Macbeth, their speeches shine),
> Why, on the verities on **thee** made good,
> May they not be my oracles as well,

And set me up in hope? But hush, no more.

Sennet sounded. Enter MACBETH *as* King, LADY MACBETH
as Queen, LENNOX, ROSS, *lords and attendants.*

MACBETH
Here's our chief guest.

LADY MACBETH   If he had been forgotten
It had been as a gap in our great feast
And all things unbecoming.

MACBETH
Tonight we hold a solemn supper, Sir,
And I'll request **your** presence.

BANQUO   Let **your** highness
Command upon me, to the which my duties
Are with a most indissoluble tie
Forever knit.

Banquo's opening words are shockingly direct, 'Thou hast it now'.
It completely denies to Macbeth the respect for his new status as
king. Shakespeare again uses the convention of **thou** use to absent
addressees to expose a character's hidden feelings. He then contrasts
this directness with Banquo's change of tack as soon as Macbeth
enters. He switches to **you**, of course, but he also starts addressing
Macbeth as 'highness' – and continues to call him 'majesty' and 'my
lord' for the rest of the scene.

Much Ado About Nothing Act 3 Scene 1, 107–16.

BEATRICE
What fire is in mine ears? Can this be true?
Stand I condemned for pride and scorn so much?

Contempt, farewell, and maiden pride adieu!

No glory lives behind the back of such.

And, Benedick, love on, I will requite **thee**,

Taming my wild heart to **thy** loving hand.

If **thou** dost love, my kindness shall incite **thee**

To bind our loves up in a holy band;

For others say **thou** dost deserve, and I

Believe it better than reportingly.

Exit

We have seen how Beatrice refuses to use **thou** to Benedick throughout the play, even when she admits her love for him and he believes himself to be her acknowledged suitor. Here, in this soliloquy, Beatrice talks to Benedick in his absence and lets her true feelings pour out. Bowled over by what she has just heard, that Benedick is in love with her, she yields to the most surprising declaration – not just that she welcomes him to 'love on' but that she will 'tame' her heart to his 'loving hand' and welcomes the idea of marriage, which she has so publicly scorned. It is not an easy speech for an actor because it runs so contrary to the character of Beatrice, as it has been established so far, but the **thou**s should help because they tell us that she is speaking from her heart. Shakespeare has exploited the convention of **thou** use to absent addressees to show us the unguarded Beatrice. (When Harriet Walter played Beatrice with the RSC, Hero and Ursula were watering flowers as they talked about Benedick's love for Beatrice, and they deliberately poured water on her as she hid behind a shrub, listening to them. As a result, she was dripping wet when she came to her soliloquy and she said it helped her a lot because she felt stripped of her dignity and of the protective show that she had put on of despising Benedick.)

4

Afterword

The scenes explored above are examples only. There are many more to be found, There is, for instance, the way the latent racism in *Othello* and *The Merchant of Venice* makes itself evident towards the ends of the plays, as contemptuous **thou**s are thrown at Othello and Shylock even by characters we think of as admirable. There are individual character implications, too: it is a convention of **thou** use between lovers that the man uses it first, but transgressive women use it to the men they want, even if the men are using **you** in reply. So, Goneril and Regan, in *King Lear*, both of them hoping for an adulterous affair with Edmund, use **thou** to him, though he uses **you** in return. And Titania, in her drug-induced passion for the 'ass' Bottom, uses **thou** to him, though he gives her stolid **you**s in return. And there are the **thou**s of the men who get too close: Both Sir John Falstaff and Sir Toby Belch use **thou** very freely: both unashamed scroungers, they still patronize others, entitled by their status as knights. At the same time, they are men who assert unjustified intimacy, ready to claim friendship from a man or the right to grope a woman; with every **thou** we can smell the beer on their breaths.

There is a complex set of factors for an actor to consider when s/he starts rehearsing a role. Understanding the significance of your character's **you/thou** use is important but it is unlikely to be your first consideration. The exercises in this book are designed to give you an instinctive sense for **thou**: to feel its strength on your tongue, to respond to its emotional power, to use its passion. If you can do that then you will have a special insight into character and relationships and a potent performance tool.

About the author

Penelope Freedman is a teacher and academic with a background both in linguistics and in theatre. With a first degree in Classics from Oxford, an MA in Linguistics from the University of Kent and a PhD on Shakespeare from Birmingham University, she has been a lecturer at Kent and Warwick universities, as well as at The Shakespeare Institute, University of Birmingham, UK. She has also directed several Shakespeare productions and played eight of Shakespeare's heroines. As Penny Freedman, she is also the author of a series of crime novels with Shakespearian themes.